Design is art people use.

OBSOLETE OBJECT
Design: George Moore
Model: Alexis Peskine

All photography:
Nancy Froehlich

BLEACHED TEXT
Design: Kim Bost
Model: Sonam Sapra

FOLLOW THESE INSTRUCTIONS TO A TEE
*Design and Model:
Alissa Faden*

MAKE IT FIT
Design: Nancy Froehlich
Model: Avelina Dougan

**YOU ARE WHERE
YOU WORK**
Design: Spence Holman
Model: Jonathan Savenilch

BARCODE
Design: Jessica Rodríguez
Model: Nathan Lotfy

BITMAP ALIEN
Design: Adam Palmer
Model: Elina Asanti

DE-BRANDED
Design: Chris Jackson
Model: Adam Savermilch

D.I.Y. Design it Yourself

Ellen Lupton, **EDITOR**
MARYLAND INSTITUTE
COLLEGE OF ART

Kimberly Bost
Michelle Brooks
Katherine Cornelius
Alissa Faden
Nancy Froehlich
Davina Grunstein
Allen Harrison
J. Spence Holman
Christopher Jackson
Julia Lupton
Josh Malinow
George Moore
Adam Palmer
Jennifer Cole Phillips
Jessica P. Rodríguez
Zvezdana Rogic
Veronica Semeco
Kristen Spilman
Mike Weikert
Jennifer Williams
Ida Woldemichael

PRINCETON
ARCHITECTURAL
PRESS

New York

Contents

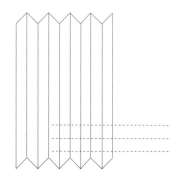

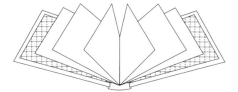

Published by
Princeton Architectural Press
37 East Seventh Street
New York, New York 10003

For a free catalog of books, call 1.800.722.6657.
Visit our web site at www.papress.com.

For more information on D.I.Y.,
visit www.designityourself.org.

© 2006 Princeton Architectural Press
All rights reserved.
Printed and bound in China.

09 08 07 06   4 3 2 1 First edition

Library of Congress Cataloging-in-Publication Data
D.I.Y. : design it yourself / edited by Ellen Lupton.
    p. cm. — (Design briefs)
ISBN 1-56898-552-5 (alk. paper)
1. Graphic arts. 2. Do-it-yourself work.
I. Lupton, Ellen. II. Series.
NC997.D59 2005
741.6—dc22
                                    2005025319

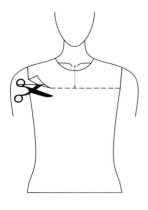

PRINCETON ARCHITECTURAL PRESS

Mark Lamster, EDITOR

Lauren Nelson, PROOFREADER

SPECIAL THANKS TO
Nettie Aljian, Dorothy Ball,
Nicola Bednarek, Janet Behning,
Becca Casbon, Penny (Yuen
Pik) Chu, Russell Fernandez,
Jan Haux, Clare Jacobson, John
King, Mark Lamster, Nancy
Eklund Later, Linda Lee, Katharine
Myers, Scott Tennent, Jennifer
Thompson, Paul Wagner,
Joseph Weston, Tiffany Wey,
and Deb Wood
—*Kevin C. Lippert,* PUBLISHER

MARYLAND INSTITUTE COLLEGE OF ART

Ellen Lupton, EDITOR

Nancy Froehlich, DIRECTOR OF PHOTOGRAPHY

Mike Weikert, STYLE POLICE

*Mike Weikert, Nancy Froehlich, and
Kristen Spilman,* COVER DESIGN

Joel Bobeck, COVER MODEL

Kristen Spilman, INSIDE COVERS

Dan Meyers, ADDITIONAL PHOTOGRAPHY

TYPEFACES
Thesis family, designed by Lucas de Groot

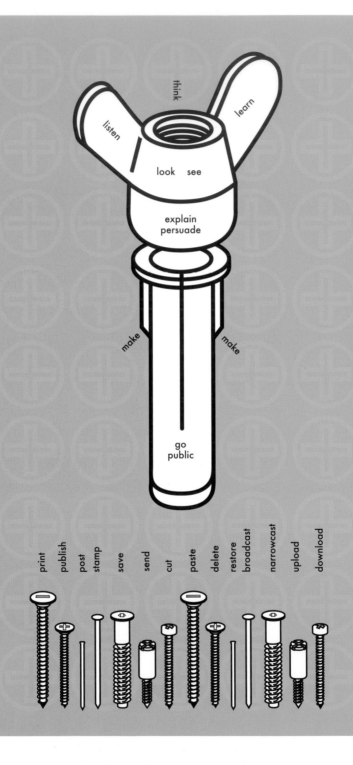

Foreword

Ellen Lupton

Design is an instrument for packaging ideas and making them public. People who have access to design tools can make tangible their own knowledge and concepts. This active mode of literacy folds back into the ability to read and understand what's out there in the world. Learning to build your own Web site, or edit your own movie, or publish your own book, makes you more critical of the media you see and read each day, and more cognizant of the skill and artistry required to create such media at the highest level.

This book was created by students and faculty in the Graphic Design MFA program at Maryland Institute College of Art (MICA) in Baltimore. Most of the design work featured on these pages was created by MICA students and faculty; also featured are selected pieces by invited guests and by independent designers whom we interviewed. Many friends from across the MICA campus shared their work and served as models and muses.

This collaborative project, which is itself a manifestation of democratic processes, celebrates graphic design as a medium of public communication that should be accessible to everyone. The ability to publish is one of the key privileges of a free society. Herein, we offer tools for thinking and making that aim to advance design as a common language.

Illustration: Bernard Canniffe

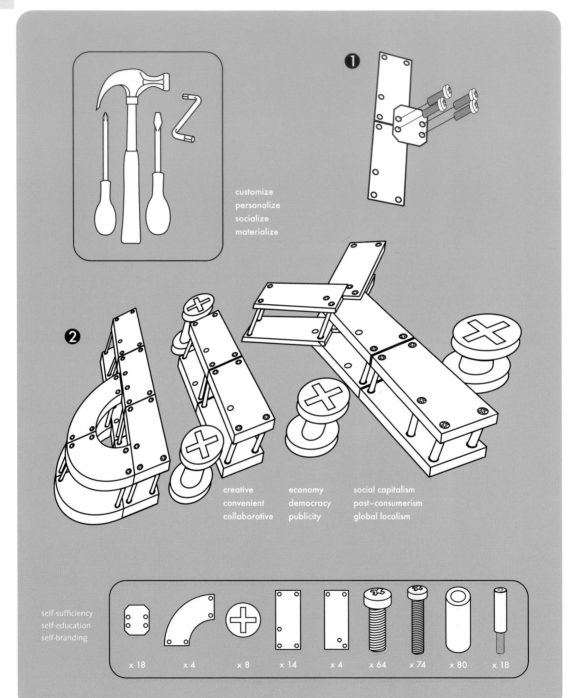

customize
personalize
socialize
materialize

1

2

creative   economy   social capitalism
convenient   democracy   post–consumerism
collaborative publicity   global localism

self-sufficiency
self-education
self-branding

x 18   x 4   x 8   x 14   x 4   x 64   x 74   x 80   x 18

Why D.I.Y.?

Ellen Lupton

This book is for people from all walks of life who want to publish words, images, and ideas on paper, on t-shirts, on the Web, or anywhere else. Current technologies—from digital fonts and the Internet to full-service copy centers—make it possible for nearly anyone to produce their own graphics. Technology alone, however, is not enough. If you learn how to think like a designer, you will be able to clarify your ideas and pull together the materials, services, and software you need to make your concepts real. This book demystifies the technical side of small-scale publishing in various media while opening up your mind to the creative side of design.

PUBLIC This book is about producing media for a public. Your public could be large or small, intimate or anonymous. Consider, for example, a t-shirt. You get up in the morning and put on a shirt with a message on it. Throughout the day, people might recognize the band, the brand, or the style printed on your clothes. The people who see your shirt—friends, family, and strangers—are your public.

People get most of their shirts from stores. Buying shirts and other products is one way of engaging the world of design. Deciding what styles you like, or what messages you want to share with other people, or what bands or companies you want to advertise on your chest, are all decisions about design and communication.

When you create your own shirt graphics, you decide exactly what you want to say and how you want to say it. You could make more than one shirt and sell them to other people, or you could give them away or trade them for other stuff you want. You could post your design on the Internet so that people could download it for free and use it themselves.

One day, you will walk down the street and see someone you don't know wearing your shirt. You will have reached your public in a new way.

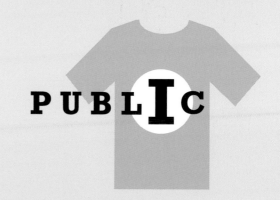

Illustrations: Bernard Canniffe

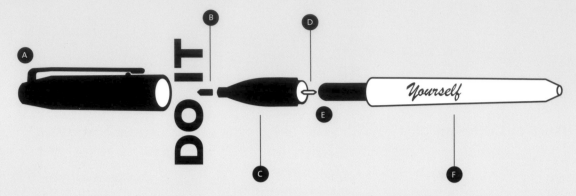

DO-IT-YOURSELF is everywhere. Around the world, people are making things themselves in order to save money, to customize goods to suit their exact needs and interests, and to feel less dependent on the corporations that manufacture and distribute most of the products and media we consume. On top of these practical and political motivations is the pleasure that comes from developing an idea, making it physically real, and sharing it with other people.

Imagine a band whose members all have day jobs. They want to promote their music, but they can't afford to hire a publicist or design agency. One guy in the band has a great visual sense, although he has never called himself a designer. (Let's call him Bob.) He does awesome marker drawings and likes to write and draw on the band's jackets. At shows, he's often asked to write on other people's clothes.

If Bob could make a poster and figure out how to get it printed, the band would save money they didn't have in the first place. If they could transfer ideas from Bob's poster to other media (press kit, CD packages, stickers, t-shirts), they would be building their own unique visual brand, one that expresses the personality of their group. They could make a Web site where people could download songs along with Bob's graphics.

Having learned to do this stuff once, they have the power to change it whenever they need to. And maybe they will want to help the start-up candy store down the street learn to produce their own graphics, too.

For people who have grown up in the digital world, the impulse to make and share one's own media is second nature. Using the Web, artists and writers publish everything from full-fledged on-line magazines to first-person blogs. Rising dissatisfaction with the music industry has led some recording artists to sell CDs directly to consumers via the Internet, bypassing the costly layers of promotion, distribution, and retailing that constitute the traditional music business.

The D.I.Y. movement relies on and stimulates public dialogue. The techniques of self-sufficiency are expounded in countless books, magazines, workshops, and Web sites. People learning new skills often want to share them with others, as seen in Web sites featuring homegrown tutorials on design, animation, and other subjects, as well as online forums, chat rooms, and bulletin boards where visitors can learn from each other. In the process of sharing their practical know-how with other people, they build a community of individuals joined together around shared interests.

DESIGN is art that people use. From the house you live in to the clothes you wear to the magazines you read, every human-made object has been designed. Graphic design is a particular area of design practice. Conveying ideas with words and pictures, graphic designers create logos, books, magazines, packages, posters, Web sites, film titles, signage, and other media.

Most professional designers studied design in an art school or university art department. This book is no substitute for such training, and it makes no claim that it will turn you into a design professional. (We do hope that some readers will be inspired to study our field in more depth.)

As a D.I.Y. design guide, this book will show you how to mobilize some of the technical and visual languages of design for use in your own life—to spread your own ideas or to promote your own band, club, church, school, or community group, or simply to make interesting things to wear and share with your friends. If you get really good at doing it for yourself, other people might ask you to do it for them, and you will be on your way to becoming a designer in the professional sense.

WHY THIS BOOK NOW? This book was produced by students and faculty in the Master of Fine Arts program at Maryland Institute College of Art (MICA). We hope to broaden design awareness by spreading knowledge of what we do.

Compared to law, medicine, or architecture, whose formal discourses date back to antiquity, graphic design is a newcomer to the professional scene, appearing in the early twentieth century. As a medium closely connected to popular culture, graphic design has had a tough time defining itself as an autonomous academic discourse. One could say that for graphic design, the barbarians have always been at the gate. We *are* the barbarians, the bastard children of the fine arts. We are the publicists and popularizers, the people of the street. You don't need a license or a set of initials after your name to become a graphic designer. Indeed, you don't need special permission from anyone to put something on paper, or on a shirt, or on the World Wide Web (as long as it's your own work or in the public domain).

Public interest in design has grown over the past twenty-five years. The rise of "desktop publishing" in the 1980s delivered digital design tools to the general public. Although some designers worried that secretaries equipped with Times Roman and Microsoft Word would obliterate the design profession, the field got bigger rather than smaller. Not only could administrative assistants bring visual order to internal publications, but managers were starting to shape their own documents, and were even becoming their own secretaries, just as graphic designers had become their own typesetters and paste-up artists. The processes of production were bubbling up through the corporate soil.

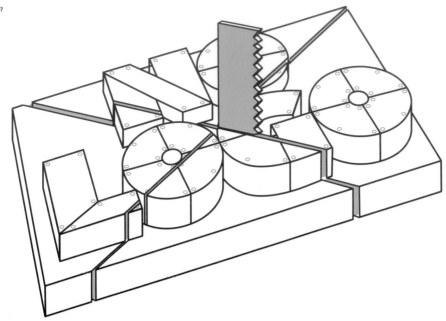

Desktop publishing made people more attentive to design values. Learning to edit and format text electronically helped them recognize the quality of professionally produced design and typography. As the cost of print production went down, expectations for design went up. Everything from memos to flyers to in-house newsletters could now be executed with some level of sophistication instead of being shoved out naked into the world. Some of this was done in-house, but a lot of it was produced by professional designers.

In the 1990s, when desktop publishing collided head-on with the World Wide Web, design became a multimedia enterprise. PowerPoint emerged as a basic job skill for middle managers, and just about anyone could hang a virtual shingle out on the Internet.

Retailers were becoming more design-oriented as well, as Pottery Barn, Crate & Barrel, IKEA, and other companies expanded their markets by offering housewares and home furnishings that felt both contemporary and familiar. These clean, accessible products became emblems of a design-conscious yet easy-to-implement lifestyle.

A big influence in the new taste-making has been Martha Stewart, who built a small catering business into a powerful family of publications, products, and media. Her magazine, *Martha Stewart Living*, provides D.I.Y. instructions for achieving beauty and hospitality in the home. Martha Stewart's editorial sensibility influenced other magazines as well as numerous catalogs and Web sites, from Williams-Sonoma to Home Depot. Inspired by Martha Stewart but seeking to express new points of view, magazines like *Real Simple*, *Readymade*, and *Budget Living* have each staked out their own territory in the arena of lifestyle publishing.

Growing alongside the awareness of design has been an anti-consumerist discourse, exemplified by the Canadian magazine *Ad Busters* and the book *No Logo*, written by the Canadian critic Naomi Klein. Raging against the corporate machine, these publications gave voice to communities of citizens disgusted by the exploitation of international workers and the destruction of natural resources represented by the endless onslaught of branding and advertising.

THREE POINTS ON THE STATE OF DESIGN TODAY

1. Many people today have achieved high levels of design awareness and visual literacy, in areas ranging from fonts to furniture.

2. Across society there is unprecedented demand for and access to the tools of self-publishing. People want to make (and share) their own media.

3. Many consumers wish to be less reliant on the corporate empire of signs, desiring to redirect the flow of consumption for their own purposes.

We have thus arrived at a compelling turn in the evolution of design consciousness. The general public is more aware than ever before of the values and languages of design, from graphics to architecture to automobiles. At the same time, many consumers, especially younger ones, distrust the global corporate economy upon which mass production relies. Furthermore, they do not identify with the gracious perfectionism of Martha Stewart or with the tidy traditionalism of Pottery Barn.

A writer whose work helped inspire the making of this book is Antonio Gramsci (1891–1937), an Italian Marxist who was jailed by the Fascist regime for the last eleven years of his life. His posthumous *Prison Notebooks* expressed a new model for the socially engaged thinker, whom he called the "organic intellectual." In contrast to the "traditional intellectuals," who were tied to formal entities such as the church, the state, the academy, and the mainstream media, the new "organic intellectuals" were doing their work in the context of trade unions, clubs, cafes, political parties, the independent press, and other emerging institutions.[1]

These organic intellectuals could merge physical and mental labor, building "new modes of thought" out of acts of doing and making. Their skills would be both technical and theoretical. To start an independent newspaper, for instance, requires knowledge of how papers are printed and distributed as well as knowledge of how to write.

Gramsci argued that all people are intellectuals, but that only some take on the public role of an intellectual within society. Likewise, we might say that everyone is a designer (a particular kind of intellectual), because all people make decisions about their environment, their personal appearance, their media consumption, and so forth. To manipulate the messages and materials of design in an active, public way is to take on the social role of the designer. Following Gramsci, we prefer to define design as a *social* function, rather than as a profession or an academic discipline.

Gramsci believed that organic intellectuals would emerge from institutions of practical learning, where thinking and doing are connected. These organic thinkers function, in turn, to educate others: they inform, explain, persuade, inspire, organize, promote, and instruct, engaging in a process of exchange and interaction through which publics are built.

The authors of this book, a group of graduate students and faculty, have each brought a body of experience to the editorial table. By asking what other people might want to know about what we do, we have expanded our own knowledge.

1. Antonio Gramsci, "The Intellectuals," *Selections from the Prison Notebooks*, ed. Q. Hoare and G. N. Smith (New York: International Publishers, 1971), p3–23.

JULIA REINHARD LUPTON

Professor of English and Comparative Literature
The University of California, Irvine
www.ThinkingWithShakespeare.org
jrlupton@uci.edu

Director, Humanities Out There
www.humanities.uci.edu/hot/
for HOT information and assistance,
call Peggie Winters, 949.824.9735

*Business card designed
by Julia Lupton
Photography: Dan Meyers*

D.I.Y. Theory

Julia Lupton

At home in post-urban California, my family battles mass mediation by playing music, making art, and designing stuff. Our desktop printers pump out everything from CD labels and birthday invitations to conference posters, classroom exercises, and graphs and charts for scholarly books. We are not designers in the professional sense, yet everyone in the house engages in daily acts of making and publishing.

Recently, I designed my own BUSINESS CARD. I can print the cards out at home on letter-sized stationery stock and trim them with a rotary paper cutter. Each sheet folds in half and slips into a small glassine envelope, the kind used by stamp collectors. Each card looks and feels like a little letter, addressed to myself but also to my several worlds. One side refers to where I work, at the University of California, Irvine, and the other side refers to my so-called private life.

I designed the card with guidance from Ellen Lupton (my twin sister and editor of this book). I wanted a card that would help me build relationships both inside and outside the university. And I wanted to do it myself, bypassing the official seal and standard typography regulated by my employer. I wanted something professional but not institutional, a tiny calling card that would fold together my several interests and identities.

As little kids, my twin and I shared a double flare for visual and verbal expression, but we decided to divide the creative pie in high school. Ellen pursued the visual arts (but found herself drawn early on towards typography). Meanwhile, I went for literature, philosophy, and foreign languages (but remained attracted to art history).

Some years later, when I began thinking about literature and citizenship, Ellen was starting to think about the public uses of graphic design. We were both, in our own ways, thinking about the social dimensions of our fields. We recently started a blog about using design in daily life.

On the following pages are short texts that link the practical aims of graphic design with a set of ideas (*public*, *capital*, *property*) that carry real weight in contemporary discussions of what it means not only to be *part of* a public, but also to *have* a public, to address an audience through acts of deliberate, designed, expression.

DESIGN-YOUR-LIFE.ORG
This card was created to promote a blog about applying design principles to problems in everyday living. *Designed by Ellen and Julia Lupton*

Ellen and Julia Lupton, EDITORS

8. Lubricate versal arms a

design-your-life.org

blog

Political culture arises out of delicate networks of mentalities and convictions that cannot be generated by or simply steered through administrative measures.

—JÜRGEN HABERMAS, *"The Destruction of Reason,"* 1991

PUBLIC A company goes public when it decides to sell its shares on the stock market. In the financial world, going public is an economic rite of passage, a kind of corporate coming out party, when a fiscal body is exposed to the judgments of the world.

A public, unlike a market, does not simply buy goods for its own use, but is involved in some discussion of the Good more generally. The Good might be ethical or political, but it can also be about style, as long as it involves a *common* good, engaging and connecting a group of people around a shared concern. Contemporary philosopher Jürgen Habermas calls this common conversation the *public sphere*. The public sphere (unlike the state and the economy, though it borders on both) is the forum where opinions are formed about what matters to a particular group of people, be it musical or mystical, ecological or culinary, athletic or aesthetic.[1]

Publics come in many sizes, from The Public at Large to fringe audiences that gel around special interests and tastes. The Internet breeds new micro-publics and counter-publics, but it also drives broader processes of opinion formation and of mass marketing. Publics are brought into being by communicative acts that grab attention, set a mood, and state a position. When an idea or opinion changes hands, there is the chance of further dissemination, of "getting the word out." Such exchanges make publics grow. Through the circulation of images and ideas, publics not only expand in size, but also become more focused and responsive social bodies.

In the context of this book, publishing is the risky, even risqué, act of sharing a document or artifact with an audience. Whether you are designing a T-SHIRT, a BUSINESS CARD, or a BLOG, you are artfully aiming your communication at a public. Whom do you want to reach (and do you care if other people are listening, too)? What opinion are you trying to form (for yourself, and for others)? What is the rhetoric, the persuasive angle and style, of your design?

Your public might be as small as a listserve or as vast as the World Wide Web. You might go public for economic reasons (selling a product, angling for a job, landing a contact), or for political ones (pushing a cause, supporting a candidate, arguing a point). But you might also have social and aesthetic motives for going public: to share your likes and dislikes, to define your style, to brand your attitude, to blog your day. In any case, you are shaping the ideas and values that matter to a public, to your public.

Publics great and small are unpredictable. You can imagine, identify, target, or massage an "ideal public," but you cannot establish with any certainty who will compose the actual public you will reach. The borders of a public are impossible to police, prone to both no-shows and party-crashing. When you go public with a product or a message, you never know who is listening, or what they will make of it themselves.

1. Jürgen Habermas, "The Destruction of Reason," *Die Zeit,* May 17, 1991.

Social capital refers to connections among individuals....
A society of many virtuous but isolated individuals
is not necessarily rich in social capital.

—ROBERT PUTNAM, *Bowling Alone*, 2000

CAPITAL Karl Marx defined capitalism as "the circulation of money as an end in itself." Capital is distinct from buying things in order to use or enjoy them. It is also different from the mere accumulation of wealth, which "petrifies money into a hoard."[2] Capital is restless, always on the move. Capital works by separating ownership from labor. The capitalist owns the means of production and distribution (the factory, the tools, the retail stores), while the worker does the producing (earning a wage instead of owning what he or she makes).

When you design your own products and publications, you get to engage both creatively and critically with capital. You can embrace the productive possibilities of capital while finding places to fracture the corporate monopoly of style and short-circuit the widening divide between production and consumption. D.I.Y. designers ride the waves of capital while seeking out new counter-currents on surfboards that sport their own imprints.

For example, creating your own BRAND (applied to a T-SHIRT, a BUSINESS CARD, or a WEB SITE) brings variety to the mass-mediated ad-scape. It also makes you think about how brands are put together, which ones work, and for whom. The D.I.Y. designer is a "producer" in both the laboring sense (you're doing the work yourself) and the Hollywood sense: you're underwriting the costs,

launching the product, and maybe collecting a profit, too. By recombining ownership and labor, you are both the capitalist and the worker in your own cottage industry.

Social theorists have applied the economic concept of capital to other forms of value.[3] *Social capital* refers to the resources you earn by networking with other people. Social capital is built by sharing food, throwing parties, giving gifts, scratching backs, and returning phone calls. Like economic capital, social capital consists of acts of exchange. It has a short shelf life, and it can't be hoarded. If you don't use it, you lose it.

Social capital is often inherited: the children of the rich or the highly educated benefit enormously from the contacts and connections of their parents. But social capital does not rest with the elite alone. Young people often determine trends in music, fashion, and language, even though they do not form the wealthiest segment of society. Immigrant communities support local businesses and find means of morphing and mixing languages and customs in order to build bridges among different groups.

Social capital can be made as well as inherited. You earn social capital by meeting people, joining groups, and getting your name out there. You can use the tools of design and publication to establish an artistic, intellectual, and social identity. D.I.Y. designers make products that help them communicate and network with other people and groups. Practicing design develops your technical capacities and increases your stylistic and aesthetic fluency. And if you really get into it, you can help your friends and associates learn how to make stuff, too, further democratizing the channels of social capital.

2. Karl Marx, *Capital: A Critique of Political Economy*, trans. Samuel Moore and Edward Aveling (New York: International Publishers, 1967), I: 249-50.

3. Robert Putnam, *Bowling Alone: The Collapse and Revival of American Community* (New York: Simon and Schuster, 2000).

PROPERTY   Property defines who we are.
Hundreds of years ago, the Enlightenment
philosopher John Locke explained that people
could make their own property by "mixing nature
with labor." [4] In contemporary consumer culture,
people express themselves through what they
own, but the things they buy are usually made
by other people. In the global economy, the
design, production, marketing, distribution, and
consumption of objects usually occur far away
from each other, at the hands of disconnected sets
of workers.

D.I.Y. design lets you look at property in a
new way. D.I.Y. designers live in a landscape
encrusted with images. The D.I.Y. designer is still
a consumer. You can't become a producer without
buying some tools. When you use PhotoShop
or Dreamweaver, you're not cooking with raw
ingredients, but rather appropriating images,
styles, and techniques already stamped with a
considerable dose of pre-packaged personality.

After the printing press was invented in the
fifteenth century, publishers, authors, and lawyers
began debating the ownership of words and ideas.
Did a play or poem belong to the author or to the
printer or to the public at large? Copyright law
became stable in the eighteenth and nineteenth
centuries, and then went into crisis again at the
end of the twentieth. Digital media presented vast
new opportunities for the corporate production
and distribution of mass media, but also for the
new cottage industries and sub-cultures of self-
publishing and file-sharing.

4. John Locke, *Second Treatise
on Government*, S. 27. Ed. Peter
Laslett (Cambridge University
Press, 1960).

NATURE

+

LABOR

=

PROPERTY

*Whatsover then he removes out of
the State that Nature hath provided,
and left it in, he hath mixed his
Labour with, and joyned to something
that is his own, and thereby makes
it his Property.*

JOHN LOCKE, *Second Treatise on Government, 1689*

FAIR USE Publication of works that are not in the public domain may fall under "fair use." The Copyright Act of 1976, 17 U.S.C. Section 107, states that fair use depends upon four factors:

1. The purpose and character of the use, including whether such use is for nonprofit educational purposes;
2. The nature of the copyrighted work;
3. The amount and substantiality of the portion used in relation to the copyrighted work as a whole; and
4. The effect of the use upon the potential market for or value of the copyrighted work.

D.I.Y. designers are hungry for fresh new images and sounds. What can you legally use, and what can't you? Most materials over seventy years old are in the *public domain*. This means that their copyright has expired and they now can be used by anyone. Public documents, including many photographs, maps, and other materials housed in the Library of Congress, belong to the American people and are available for your use. (See www.loc.gov.)

What kind of place is this "public domain"? To some, the public domain is a necropolis, or city of the dead, into which works of art "fall" when they are no longer profitable. If certain works can maintain their profitability, goes the reasoning among this group, then their copyright should be extended in order to save them from falling into this dead zone.

But this dead zone is in fact a ground of public life, more like the "free range" or common grazing lands of the Old West. Ranchers needed their cattle to roam across open areas that belonged to no one, while farmers wanted to clear and fence stretches of this public land for more intensive private use.[5] Self-publishers are digital cowboys, thriving on flexible, low-use access to a vast territory of content. Professional publishing is more like homesteading, requiring clear property lines in order to maximize yields from a small, highly worked set of materials.

5. See Robert A. Baron, "Making the Public Domain Public," http://www.studiolo.org/IP/VRA-TM-SF-PublicDomain.htm.

Libraries, schools, and universities have tried to establish workable guidelines for fair use (see above). The main thing to keep in mind is that if you are turning a profit using someone else's words, images, or music, you need to get permission to use the materials. If you are not aiming to make a profit, you still need to acknowledge your sources.

As a producer of designed communication, you also have certain rights to your own work. No one should be able to make a profit from your stuff without your permission, and your creative work should be acknowledged in any public use of it. If you believe in a broad and accessible public domain, you can release all or some of your rights by posting a Creative Commons License through CreativeCommons.org. This group offers a flexible set of licensing and copyright models for your own work, with an emphasis on promoting a generous definition of the public domain that encourages collaboration and creativity among digital self-publishers.

OPEN SOURCE · OPEN HOUSE · OPEN FOR BUSINESS · DESIGN

THE GENIUS OF SEEING THAT WHICH IS SO EVIDENT AS TO BE UNSEEABLE

POSTER CONTEST
FALL 2004

In collaboration with:

JUDGES

Art Chantry / Ellen Lupton
James Victore

POSTER 4 IN A SERIES OF 4

Design / *Tristan Benedict-Hall*
Quote / *Daniel Quinn*

Silkscreened on French Paper / Construction 80 lb. / Slate Blue

For more information visit *underconsideration.com/poster*

Basic design

Jennifer Cole Phillips

The best design almost seems effortless. Like a great song or stylish pair of shoes, we sense the whole effect rather than the individual parts and process that went into the making. Whether product, printed page, or present for a friend, design inspires, incites, impresses, and informs. This chapter offers basic principles and techniques to help guide your work and give your projects punch!

FROM THE INSIDE TO THE OUTSIDE
Before considering formal issues such as layout, color, and typefaces, think about who you want to speak to and what you want to say. Once you're clear on these goals, an appropriate visual solution can grow in response. Begin with a dissection of your project. What is the subject matter? Who is your audience? What is the purpose? Do some brainstorming on paper to answer these questions, and you will be on your way to finding the appropriate voice for your design.

I like a lot the adage that for every problem there is a solution that is simple, obvious, and wrong. A problem worthy of the name is seldom accessible to sudden and simple solution.
—MALCOLM GREAR

SUBJECT + AUDIENCE + PURPOSE = VOICE
Did you ever notice how your spoken voice and mannerisms fluctuate depending on with whom you are talking? You may brighten your tone and exaggerate detail when speaking to a child; deepen and intensify it when angry; soften it while sharing a secret. These instinctive responses remind us how much impact audience has on our behavior. The same logic applies in a design context—in order to communicate effectively, your design must speak with the appropriate voice for your subject, audience, and purpose. For instance, a big, crude font and crowded composition wouldn't make sense for a Zen tea house menu. Similarly, a slender, san-serif font composed in a sparse field would fail to conjure the right feel for a pit beef joint.

GETTING BEYOND THE FAMILIAR People, places, thoughts, and things become familiar through repeated exposure. For this reason, the first ideas that pop into your head are generally ideas that you have experienced many times before. Take the time to think beyond the familiar—your fresh ideas will pique and hold people's attention.

SPEAK UP POSTER
Hand drawn letters have been carefully embedded in their surrounding field to reinforce the message.
Design:Tristan Benedict-Hall

Right and wrong do not exist in graphic design. There is only effective and non-effective communication.

—PETER BILAK

HIERARCHY Once you've decided what you want to say, the first formal task is to determine a clear hierarchy: that is, the order in which elements will be emphasized. When design elements are too evenly weighted, the audience quickly loses interest. This happens because the designer has not provided clear visual cues to help readers navigate the content.

Designing a hierarchy is both an intuitive and logical process. Like sound, elements that command our attention tend to be louder, separating themselves by their emphatic quality or location. Devices used to create emphasis include increased size, weight, and color. The hierarchy enables each level of emphasis or respective category (title, text, captions, images) to stand clearly apart from every other category.

VISUAL PATH Effective compositions often have a major focal point — typically an image, whether photographic or illustrative — that appears larger and more emphatic than any other element in that environment. To direct the viewer's eye through the design, carefully distribute elements to create balance, tension, and movement.

WHITE SPACE Have you ever looked through a magazine and been struck by an almost empty page with just one element on it? Like a whisper in the whir of noise and shouting, a simple page catches our attention not by shouting but by restraint. Think of white space as you do any visual element—notice and control the shape, volume, and placement to add emphasis and impact. Like good writing, the art of using white space involves what's left out as much as what's left in.

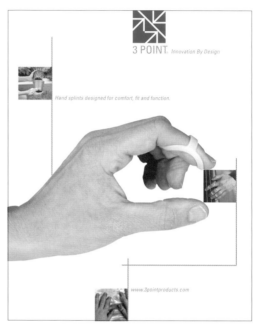

HIERARCHY, FOCAL POINT, VISUAL PATH, AND ASYMMETRICAL BALANCE
The splinted hand, silhouetted for contrast and compositional interest, forms the central focal point, while the other elements create a consistent but subordinate layer below. Placement and repetition of the squares and rules help create balance, tension, and movement through the space.
Design: J. Cole Phillips

SCALE AND CROPPING
Enlarge or reduce your subject in unexpected ways. Crop out unnecessary detail and try bleeding images off edges—this helps achieve depth of field and adds interest.

SYMMETRY AND ASYMMETRY are two strategies for achieving compositional balance. Symmetrical design is oriented on a central axis: the right side is a mirror image of the left. This technique lends stability and is often used in more formal communications like wedding invitations and announcements. Asymmetrical design is organic and achieves tension and order through the uneven distribution and balance of type, images, and color in space. Generally speaking, asymmetrical design attracts and holds your audience's attention longer because the visual relationships are not optically predictable.

CONTRAST is among the most potent tools a designer can use to create impact and emphasis. Types of contrast are limited only by one's imagination. To name a few:

big/small	*tall/wide*
soft/hard	*in-motion/static*
transparent/opaque	*many/few*
thick/thin	*smooth/rough*
organic/structured	*color/monochromatic*

When you juxtapose an element with its opposite, the inherent qualities of that element stand out more dramatically, thereby increasing the overall dynamic of the design.

IMAGES bring publications to life. When you create or crop images, several principles will help convey a stronger, clearer visual point-of-view. First, compose or crop with an eye for bold, graphic form, high contrast, and clear color.

When denoting context, include only enough visual information to establish that context. Showing part of a dog and not the entire dog will still say dog, yet may make a more interesting image. Experiment with scale— make something huge that's ordinarily tiny and vice versa. Try capturing your subject from a surprising angle— from above, underneath, even inside out.

COLOR is a powerful communicator. More than perhaps any other visual element, color can set the mood or signal a subject area. Red is dynamic and often associated with passion or violence; blue can be calm or authoritative (think jazz and blue suits); green evokes the environment and health, and yellow is optimistic and warm. Use color with discretion—one or two colors can have more impact than many, and such restraint often has the added benefit of being more economical to print.

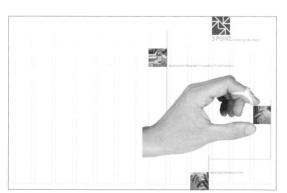

UNDERLYING GRID
A grid acts like a skeleton, providing structural support for your type and images. Build a grid when opening a new document by specifying the margins, number of columns, and gutter width.

Blogs

Christopher Jackson

Blogs have opened up the public discourse about design and politics as well as amplifying the daily musings of individuals. A blog can serve as a forum for a single person or for a larger community. With a little planning you, too, can let the world know what's one your mind, and for very little money. Depending on your desired level of control and access to technology, your blog can be edited entirely by you, or it can incorporate comments and contributions from readers. A blog can be a simple text-only site, or it can function like an illustrated digital newspaper.

GETTING STARTED Blogs come in many forms, from sophisticated design forums to places where parents brag about their kids. Blogs, short for "Web logs," are a modification of Internet message boards, whose relentlessly linear construction makes them difficult to navigate. Blogs are designed to make it easy for authors to post information and for readers to follow the thread of on-line conversations.

Like diaries, most blogs are abandoned soon after they are begun, and most are interesting primarily to their own authors. A successful blog, however, can become an important destination for a given public, from the members of an organized trade to the members of an extended family.

Many services exist that allow people to quickly and easily set up their own blogs, without requiring any special software or technical knowledge. Experienced Web designers use programs such as Movable Type to build more complex, interactive blogs from scratch.

Although blogs typically express the thoughts of an individual, some blogs are participatory and interactive, with articles posted by a core group of contributors and responses posted by readers.

Begin your endeavor by planning the subject matter and editorial feel of your blog. Will you be the town representative on local events and gossip, or will you represent a far-flung network of bottle-cap collectors?

DESIGN AND CULTURE BLOGS
boingboing.net, designobserver.com, tsunamihelp.blogspot.com, arjanwrites.com, design-your-life.org, blogcritics.org, mike.essl.com, chattababy.com, mikeindustries.com/blog, athensmusic.com, nj.com/weblogs/music

PLANNING YOUR BLOG

• *Who is your desired audience?*

• *Is the blog about you and your opinions, or is it a community forum?*

• *What are your software and Web design skills?*

• *Will your blog be hosted on a blogging site, or will it be a free-standing Web site?*

BLOGGER Blogger.com's automated system provides simple tools and Web space for your daily posts. Getting started requires zero capital and minimal technical knowledge. Templates allow for logo placement and banner changes. With time and expertise, other graphic images can be integrated into your blog.

FREE BLOG HOSTING

The simplest way to start blogging is to open an account on a hosting site such as Blogger.com. These sites provide design templates and a simple user interface for postings. "Free" packages will demand that some form of advertising appears on your page; for a monthly fee, these sites will allow you to have ad-free pages.

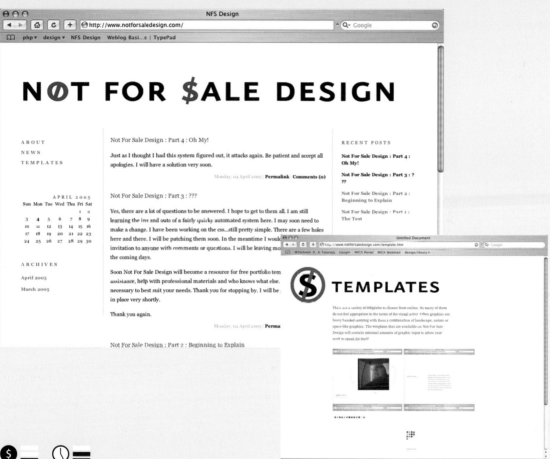

MOVEABLE TYPE

For those willing to invest more time and money developing a blog, Moveable Type is a great option. This software allows you to custom-build an interactive, two-way blog as well as creating pages free of advertising and predetermined links. Moveable Type must be installed on your Web site's server in order to function. MT also offers TypePad, a hosting service with simple, flexible templates.
Design: Christopher Jackson

Built in Moveable Type, this design blog offers free Web templates and other services to visual artists. Mildly obsessive about typography, the author wants to be able to modify the code and imagery of his blog to create a custom look.

Books (blank)

Kimberly Bost, Nancy Froehlich, and Kristen Spilman

Blank books are a refuge for you and your ideas. They can be used as sketchbooks, journals, diaries, or travel logs. They are great for taking notes, jotting down phone numbers, or generating ideas. Why not customize your blank books from conception? Numerous publications exist that detail the processes of book-binding. The introduction offered here demonstrates just how easy it is to train paper and cardboard to take the shape of a book.

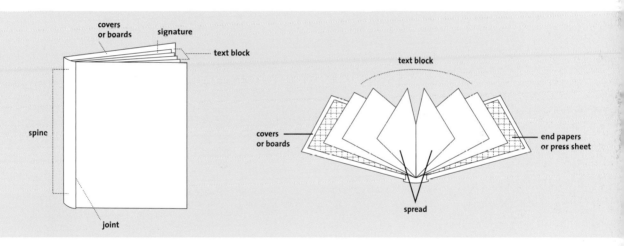

ANATOMY OF THE BOOK Multiple sheets of paper bound together comprise the blank book. Your choice of binding methods will be influenced by factors such as page count, paper weight, folding, desired durability, the quantity of books to be produced, and whether or not it is important for the book to lie flat when opened. The following pages present several ways to construct a book. Endless variations can be made to each type.

Experiment with different types of paper. Consider color, texture, pattern, weight, and found papers.

TEXT BLOCKS The core of most books is the text block, a group of pages that are sewn or glued together.Cheap paperbacks typically are glued, whereas well-made books (such as this one) are sewn. Look for the stitches in the crease between pages 40 and 41! A sewn book is made from *signatures*, groups of pages that are folded down the middle and then gathered together to make a larger text block. A book consisting of just one signature can be stapled through the centerfold.

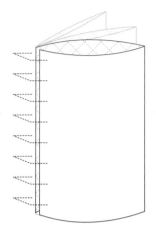

FRENCH FOLD Individual sheets of paper folded in half and bound together at the open—rather than the creased—edge are called French folds. Sheets folded this way can either be glued together or bound with a coil, posts, or stitches. This method is useful if you want to avoid double-sided printing.

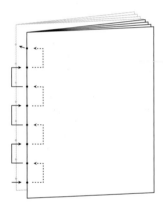

SEWN SIGNATURES Make signatures by folding four or more sheets of paper together down the center. Puncture eight evenly spaced holes in the fold of each signature. Sew along the first signature, beginning from the outside bottom hole and weaving out through the next hole. Continue this pattern until you reach the top of the signature. Attach the second signature by beginning to sew at the top hole and continuing the stitch through the bottom. Hold the signatures securely together by tying a square knot around the exposed thread along the top and bottom lines of the binding. Repeat this process until the desired text block size is bound. Books made from sewn signatures lie flat when opened.

TAPE BINDING Copy centers provide a service called tape binding, in which glue is heated and then attached to a group of pages before it cools again. The glue is concealed beneath a strip of tape. Tape-bound books are surprisingly durable, and they lie flat when opened. This method works well for binding books consisting of at least thirty pages. (The glue will seep out and spoil books with too few pages.)

To make your own tape binding, trim covers and text block to size. Tightly clamp together on three sides, leaving one side exposed for the spine. Apply three or four generous coats of PVA adhesive along exposed side, allowing each application to dry before applying the next. Conceal glue with duct tape, contact paper, or another material.

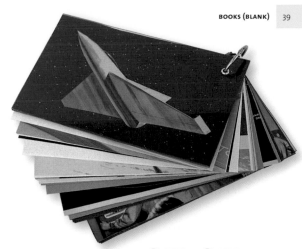

MECHANICAL BINDINGS A spiral-bound notebook and a loose-leaf binder have something in common: they both consist of single sheets of paper joined together with hardware. This makes them different from books that are made from sheets folded into signatures (see opposite page). There are several ways to construct a book out of loose sheets; each one allows you to combine different kinds of paper in a single book.

COIL BINDING

This method is economical for short-run publications as well as for making blank books. Coil-bound books lie flat when opened, which makes them enjoyable to use. Copy shops offer a variety of coil bindings. The book shown here was made with a GBC Pro-Click binding system, which consists of a compact, affordable hole puncher and plastic binding coils.
Design: Kristen Spilman

BINDER RINGS allow you to informally collect a set of blank or printed pages. Trim the covers and the paper to the same size. Place the front and back covers in position and gently tap the book on a flat surface to align the pages. Clamp the book together with butterfly clips and drill or punch a hole in the top left corner at least 1/4 inch away from the edge. Insert a binder ring. For a more finished look, attach small grommets to the front and back covers.
Design: Nancy Froehlich

BINDING STUDS

Unlike screws you would buy at a hardware store, binding studs are designed specifically for book-making. They come in several different sizes and have a closure that covers the back of the screw. Binding studs are availabe at arts-and-crafts stores. Grommets can be used in a similar way to bind books.

Trim the covers and the paper to the same size. Place the front and back covers in position and gently tap the book on a flat surface to align the pages. Clamp the book together with butterfly clips and punch two to five holes at least 1/4 inch away from the edge. (Larger books need more holes). Books bound this way do not lie flat, although horizontal formats will open better than vertical ones.
Design: Kimberly Bost

COVERS can be made from a variety of materials, adding physical as well as graphic character to your book. A few ideas are shown here.

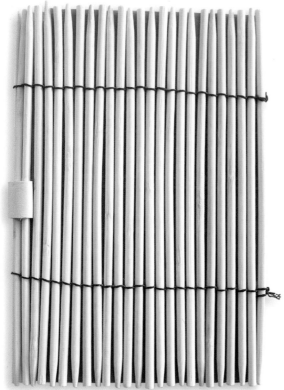

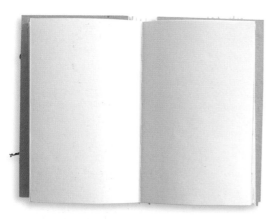

HAND SEWN CHOPSTICK

Begin with draping two strings of waxed linen thread at each end of the first stick, so that there is an equal amount of thread on either side of the stick. Secure the first stick with a single square knot on each string. Proceed with the next stick, alternating its direction and securing with a knot from each string. Repeat this process until the desired cover size is created. Adhere the chopstick cover to two panels of chip board using a hot glue gun for support. Align each panel with opposite edge of the cover, leaving enough space for the text block plus 1/8 inch in the middle. Attach the text block (made from sewn signatures) to the cover by weaving leather or ribbon through the center exposed stitch of the text block and the reserved chopstick space in middle of the cover. Secure leather/ribbon with hot glue.

PHOTO COVER

Use an old photo or personal snap shot as a cover. This book was tape bound and covered with a laminated photo that was adhered to card stock paper.

FOUND COVER

Used pages from existing books or magazines can contain fun imagery to make witty and surprising covers. The book to the left uses chip board covers that are attached together using duct tape (which acts as the spine), and then covered with pages from an old sewing book. The tape-bound text block is then glued to the endpapers.

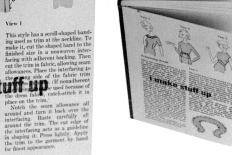

WOOD BINDER

Cut wood to desired size for covers and spine. Trim piano hinges to the same size of the cover. Use "liquid nails" to attach hinges between the covers and spine. Add an inside pocket, pen holder, and notepad using wood glue.

Books (printed)

Kimberly Bost, Nancy Froehlich, and Kristen Spilman

Few experiences are more satisfying than publishing your own words and images in the pages of a book. A printed book can serve as a professional portfolio, a collection of family photographs, or a volume of poetry. It can also have a more ephemeral life as a brochure, theater program, or zine. You can bind a single volume painstakingly by hand or employ mechanical means to produce it cheaply for wider distribution. Using page layout programs and a variety of output methods, you can put creative content into print in relatively inexpensive ways. Whether you are looking to reach five people or five hundred, we have ideas for how to get yourself published.

ARTIST'S BOOKS To create the content for this chapter, we designed books for friends who are artists. Each artist specializes in a different medium: painting, song writing, photography, and mixed media. By designing the books in response to the artists' work, we were able to test a variety of formats and binding methods.

We used some of the binding methods presented in the previous chapter as well as some new ones. Whereas the design and production of a blank book hinges largely on materials and construction methods, printed books pose additional problems of reproduction and assembly. For example, careful planning is required to set up printed pages so that they can be bound together in a signature. Below are questions to consider in deciding what type of book is appropriate for your needs.

THE STUDIO
Think of an artist's book as a miniature gallery, a portable environment for the pictures it contains.
Artist: Alexis Peskine
Photograph: Nancy Froehlich

PLANNING YOUR BOOK

• *Do the pages need to lie flat when the book is open?*

• *How many books do you need, and how many pages will there be?*

• *Does the book need to be light-weight for mailing?*

• *How much handwork is involved in producing the book?*

• *Will you be binding single sheets, multiple signatures, or French folds?*

• *Does the book need to be durable?*

• *Do you need to print on two sides of each page?*

• *What is the budget?*

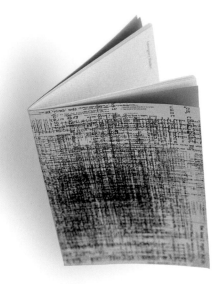

THE LYRICIST Roshan Gurusinghe is a production artist by day and lyricist/musician by night. He writes lyrics for the Seattle bands, baby i love you and "Booker Brown." Roshan wanted to present his lyrics in the format of a book. He needed at least 300 copies for various projects, and he wanted to be able to produce more books as needed. A photocopied, saddle-wired booklet was an economical solution.

A *saddle wire* is a metal stitch (like a staple) placed through the center fold of a single signature. Copy centers provide this service, or you can do it yourself with a long-necked stapler, available at office supply stores.

Saddle-wired books lie flat when opened. For the best results, keep your page count under twenty-four pages; otherwise the book will bow open around the center spread. Saddle wiring can only be used to bind a single-signature book. If you don't want the wire to show, make a paper book jacket to wrap around the cover.

When preparing files for a saddle-wired book, you must arrange your pages in printer's spreads (see NEWSLETTER chapter), because when the pages are folded and bound together, they will be in a different order from how they are designed on screen (except for the center spread). This process is also called *imposition*, the arrangement of pages for printing.

Photocopying is an affordable printing method for a relatively short-run project like this one. You can achieve a sophisticated effect by substituting standard photocopy paper with more interesting papers. We used an off-white textured card stock for the cover and a lighter-weight off-white paper for the text block. We inserted end sheets made of tinted vellum between the cover and the text block, offering an element of surprise, variation, and color as the reader opens the book.

SADDLE WIRE
The choice of paper and the careful attention to typography make this book feel both literary and experimental. Once you have invested time in designing and planning a project like this, it is easy and inexpensive to produce multiple copies.
*Design: Kimberly Bost
Photography:
Kristen Spilman*

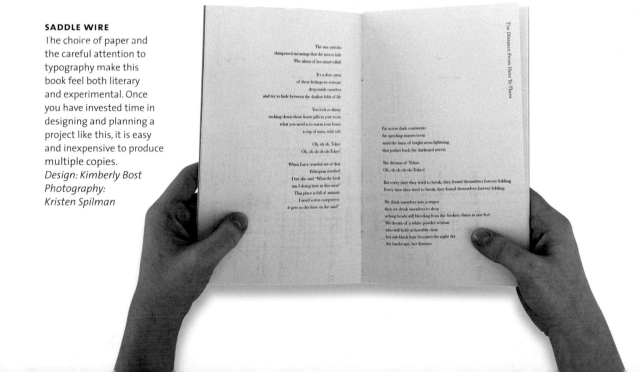

THE PAINTER Lori Larusso's recent body of work has two distinct aspects. Some of her work looks at the systematic makeup of stereotypical middle America. As a culture, we set up systems that we simultaneously disrupt, both negatively (through abuse of power and misdistribution of wealth) and positively (through free will, protest, and reciprocity). The second half of Lori's work takes the form of small, glossy paintings of petty indulgences. These images welcome the viewer's need for frivolous and immediate satisfaction within consumer culture.

Lori wanted to produce a self-promotional piece that would simultaneously show these related themes and yet keep them distinct. She needed ten books to distribute to curators and for grant proposals. An accordion-fold book mirrors the "two-fold" nature of Lori's work by permitting two bodies of work to exist separately, printed on opposite sides of the page, yet contained within one book. Reproducing her paintings demanded attention to color. We carefully monitored the output from our inkjet printer and adjusted our print settings to keep the color of the prints as close as possible to the color of the paintings.

ACCORDION FOLD LAYOUT: *side A & side B*

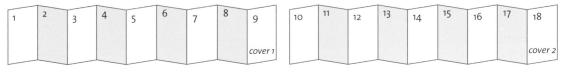

The accordion fold allows the book to function both as a poster and a book. The viewer can look at the work as one long spread or flip through page by page just like a standard book. The first page of the piece can serve as the cover, or you can attach heavier-weight covers to the front and back as an additional feature (as we did here). The covers of Lori's book were screen-printed on chip board and then attached using Xyron permanent adhesive.

ACCORDIAN FOLD
Design the book as one long spread; the last page on the right is the cover for both front and back. Print on a long sheet of double-sided paper (available from digital output services). Score and fold each page, alternating from one side to the other. Apply covers after folding. *Design and photography: Kristen Spilman*

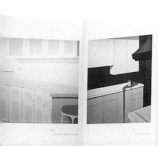

THE MIXED MEDIA ARTIST Alexis Peskine is an artist from Paris who wants to promote his work to galleries in New York. The book needs to be easy to carry around and inexpensive to mail. The solution was a 5-x-5-inch portfolio with metal binding studs that mimic the dots and nails he uses in his work.

To make the book easier to open, we sandwiched sheets of translucent vellum paper between back-to-back pairs of color prints. The vellum sheets are an inch or so longer than the prints, creating a flexible hinge towards the spine of the book. We punched holes through the vellum hinge, and we used binding studs to hold the sheets together (see previous chapter). This method allows for more flexibility when turning the page.

Design and photography:
Nancy Froehlich

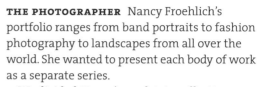

Design: Kristen Spilman
Photography: Nancy Froehlich

THE PHOTOGRAPHER Nancy Froehlich's portfolio ranges from band portraits to fashion photography to landscapes from all over the world. She wanted to present each body of work as a separate series.

We divided Nancy's work into collections and created a set of promotional books to leave behind with potential clients. By categorizing her work with broad titles such as "people" and "landscapes," she will be able to update and produce more books as her portfolio grows.

Nancy will be using her home equipment to print each book, so we chose a simple D.I.Y. binding method and added a little customization. Her books are coil-bound (see previous chapter), but the back cover is 1 1/2 times the length of the open book. The back cover wraps around to the front and forms a spine that conceals the coil.

PACIFIST BODYSUIT
All design: Mike Weikert
Model: Maya Weikert
Photography: Nancy Froehlich

pacifist

Brands

Mike Weikert

What is a brand? A brand is an idea, not a thing. It is a shifting set of perceptions and associations that can be influenced but not controlled. Memorable brands such as Altoids or Starbucks thrive on a coherent set of products and a strong, identifiable design approach. A successful brand connects to its audience on an emotional level, representing a feeling, an idea, a way of life. Use design to shape your own brand, whether its your band, team, gallery, or personal hair-cutting service.

BRAND STRATEGY This chapter looks at a real-world case study: Small Roar, my new baby clothing company. After the birth of our daughter, my wife Stephannie and I realized that new parents want to express a point of view through their baby's clothing, and we saw an opportunity to create fresh and innovative products that would appeal to other parents like us. I developed the concept as my graduate thesis project at MICA and then took it to the marketplace.

Brand Strategy is the combined understanding of your product's position in the marketplace (target audience, competition), its visual identity (from the product itself to packaging, logos, and promotional materials), and your marketing initiatives (how your product or service will be delivered to customers). These components should work together to support your business goals.

BRAND POSITIONING How does your product or service compare to your competition? What makes it unique or different? Who is your potential market? Our brand, Small Roar, is the fusion of graphic design, free speech, and baby clothes. Using the graphic t-shirt as an inexpensive way to make a visual statement, Small Roar gives babies (and their parents) a voice.

Our audience is hip, smart parents looking for an alternative to the Babies-R-Us clothing options as well as friends and family of parents looking for a clever, memorable baby gift.

BRAND IDENTITY Brand identity is the visual language that a company uses to communicate with its audience. Our brand identity reflects our marketing statement: It's not about pinks or blues, ducks or bears. It's about design culture and self-expression. It's about making a statement and wearing it loud. Most of all, it's about cool clothes for cool babies.

Our name (taken from the saying, "Keep it to a small roar"), our logo (a typographic speech bubble), and our products all make-up the foundation for our brand's visual language.

PRODUCT Your product or service is the most important part of your brand. This is what gives your public a tangible value. A well-designed product provides an immediate, emotional connection to your audience.

It is crucial to find reliable vendors capable of manufacturing your product in a high-quality and timely fashion. Key factors include material, size, color, graphics, labels, hang tags, and packaging. These elements become part of the product as it speaks to people in a sales environment.

MATERIAL
Material says a lot about your brand. Small Roar chooses to use 100% cotton, American-made, sweatshop-free garments manufactured by American Apparel. It costs a little more, but it affirms values that matter to us and to our customers. Our first collection features five conceptual designs. Each is available in two sizes: 3-6 and 6-12 months.

HANG TAG

Hang tags are attached to the garment and provide price and product information as well as your logo, tag line, and URL. The hang tag should reflect the graphic identity of your brand.

RE-LABELING

Small Roar graphics are screen-printed onto American Apparel garments, requiring us to replace the manufacturer's label with a Small Roar label. This process is known as re-labeling and is common practice.

Labels are typically woven or printed and are available in many materials, sizes, finishes, cuts and folds. Woven labels are generally taffeta or satin, and printed labels are polyester.

A label can be sewn-in under or over the seam of the garment depending on cost and desired effect. You can also silkscreen your logo directly onto the garment as an alternative to re-labeling.

We use a printed label that is the same material, color, and width as the original American Apparel label. Doing this allows us to keep the Amerian Apparel care label in tact, with size information visible to the retailer and customer.

BUSINESS CARD
By sticking a label on the back of the Small Roar hang tag, we make it double as a business card. This fun, cost-effective use of resources is appropriate for a small, independent business.

PROMOTION Promoting your company, product or service is crucial to your brand's success. If your idea is good, you need to make sure people hear about it. Whether you use direct mail, media, or word-of-mouth, it's important to get your message to your audience.

Identify local resources that might share your interest and be willing to help promote or even sell your goods. Areas of focus are publications, retail stores, institutions, and trade organizations.

POSTCARD
Postcards are a low-cost, flexible promotional tool. The Small Roar postcard features product photography and information as well as our marketing statement. We left space on the back of the card for a label that can be customized with additional information for retailers or consumers. On-line services like Modern Postcard are a source for fast, affordable mailers. For an additional fee, they will address and send your postcards.

WWW.SMALLROAR.COM
Products are the focus of
the Small Roar Web site,
which serves both retail and
wholesale customers.

DISTRIBUTION Sell. Sell. Sell. Look at building direct sales as well as your wholesale business. With direct sales, you make twice the profit and experience the joy of working directly with your customers. Secure, on-line shopping cart services, like PayPal, make setting up a store and selling your goods on-line safe and easy.

DISTRIBUTING YOUR PRODUCT

• A Web site is an efficient way to promote your brand. Create a one-stop shop where the consumer is able to learn about your company, see your product, and, most importantly, buy your stuff.

• Develop an extensive list of retailers. Where you sell is as important as what you sell from a branding perspective.

• Wholesale prices are generally half of the retail price. Consider consigning your product to get a specific store. This entails entrusting a store to sell your product without paying you upfront. They pay you as your products sell. If sales are brisk, the retailer may buy wholesale the next time around.

• When selling your product wholesale, make sure the ordering process is user-friendly. The simpler the process, the more likely the retailer will buy.

• Keep accurate records of orders and inventory. Your professionalism is a direct reflection of your brand. Besides, it will make your life a lot easier.

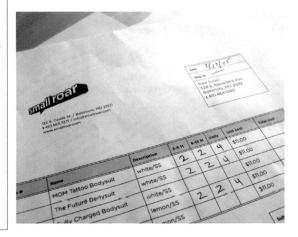

THIS IS ME!

Business cards

J. Spence Holman and Kristen Spilman

The business card remains an indispensable tool in the digital age. Cards are crucial for, well, business, but they are useful for countless other forms of networking as well. Make one for your freelance lawn ornament business, your goat farm, your band, your new baby, or just being you. Remove "business" from the title, and use your card for anything you want. In this chapter, learn how to make a card for every one of your identities.

HISTORY Business and calling cards first appeared in seventeenth-century England. Business cards acted primarily as advertising, while calling cards served as letters of introduction among the middle and upper classes. Etiquette dictated, however, that one type of card could not be substituted for the other. Today, cards are used interchangeably for social and business purposes.

STANDARD SIZE Card sizes have varied over the years, but at some point 3 1/2 x 2 inches became the norm. Consider the pros and cons when deciding on whether to deviate from the standard size. Odd shapes and sizes are attractive and memorable; consider, however, the needs of the end user. Many people use Rolodexes, business card holders and plastic sheet protectors for filing and storage, and those accessories all utilize the standard size. An odd-size card has a higher chance of ending up in the trash simply because it is inconvenient. Either way you go, there are dozens of options for creating a card that is uniquely your own. Conforming to the standard size does not have to be a limitation; rather, it is just one less decision to be made. You can also use the standard size in a creative way by orienting your card vertically instead of horizontally.

STANDARD INFORMATION Cards typically present a person's name, company name, address, phone number, e-mail, and Web address. You decide what content is right for you.

DONNAYOUNG

d_i_young@yahoo.com · 410.555.6162

PLANNING YOUR BUSINESS CARD

• *Think about how you plan to use your card when determining how much contact information to include.*

• *Maybe you want to go the mysterious route by leaving your name off and just including your Web site or e-mail address.*

• *Consider making a two-sided card, splitting your information between the front and back.*

• *Maybe your cards will serve primarily as examples of your photographs or artwork, with limited contact information.*

• *Working out of your home? You may want to set up a mailbox at the local post office for privacy.*

Photography: Nancy Froehlich

TYPOGRAPHY is the art of choosing letterforms and arranging them on a page. Using type thoughtfully is crucial to the success of your card, which will become a typographic portrait of you. Working with just a single font, you can create endless variations by playing with size, placement, and alignment (flush left, flush right, centered, or justified). The following examples are set in Helvetica and Adobe Garamond, two classic sans serif and serif typefaces.

donna i. young*

1790 Bodoni Way, Serif, MD 20175
d_i_young@yahoo.com
*ph. (410) 555-6162

- Choose a typeface that is legible at small sizes.

- Use a maximum of two different type families; most likely, you can achieve what you want with only one.

- Keep your type size between 7.5 and 10 points. Anything larger will appear clunky in the small space of the card.

- Punctuation isn't just for grammarians. Think about different ways to highlight your information. Use periods or underscores instead of hyphens and parentheses in phone numbers. Try asterisks, tildes, ampersands, slashes, etc.

- Try asymmetrical as well as symmetrical designs.

- Create a visual hierarchy of information by shifting weight, size, and case (upper and lower).

- Use a minimum of 1/8-inch margins. Anything smaller may be difficult to print correctly.

- Avoid drop shadows and other distracting effects.

- Use line spacing that appears balanced: not too tight, and not too loose.

- Great work can come from flaunting convention, but it's a good idea to know the rules before you break them.

---

donna i. young   1790 Bodoni Way, Serif, Md. 20175
d_i_young@yahoo.com
410.555.6162

---

donna i. young *graphic designer*
1790 Bodoni Way, Serif, MD 20175
d_i_young@yahoo.com / www.diydesign.com
ph. (410) 555-6162 / fax (410) 555-6163

Donna I. Young

1790 Bodoni Way
Serif, MD 20175

d_i_young@yahoo.com

ph. (410) 867-5309

D-I-YOUNG@YAHOO.COM
DONNA I. YOUNG 410-555-6162
SERIF, MD 20175
1790 BODONI WAY

D_I_YOUNG@YAHOO.COM
DONNA 1790 BODONI WAY
ISABELLE SERIF, MD 20175
YOUNG
410.555.6162

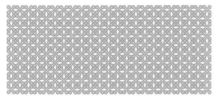

410.555.6162   DONNA I. YOUNG } d_i_ydesign@yahoo.com

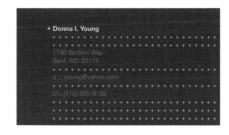

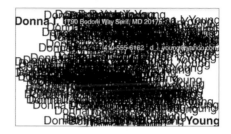

TYPE ELEMENTS Explore your keyboard. A convenient resource for interesting designs can be found, quite literally, at your fingertips. Characters such as < > / { } [ ] + ! @ % & * ( ) are great for creating patterns, icons, and emphasis. Turn over every rock you stumble upon: many characters are hidden and must be accessed with alternate keystrokes.

Most computers come equipped with **symbol** fonts like *Zapf Dingbats* or *Wingdings,* providing another great design resource. Dingbats are picture fonts that come in all shapes and sizes. Characters in Zapf Dingbats include ✢✦✪✱✳❉❖✓✘✚✎✌✈✦✈☎✠. Also consider using simple shapes like lines, squares, and circles.

COLOR can help your design stand out and come to life. At the same time, too many colors can turn into visual overload. Choose colors that represent you and your message. Also, be aware of your budget; when printing commercially, single-color or black-and-white printing is typically cheaper than full color.

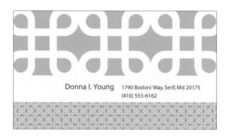

*Business cards designed by
J. Spence Holman
and Kristen Spilman*

MATERIALS Most cards are made of card stock (go figure), which is more durable than text-weight paper. Card stock withstands bending, tearing and crumpling, and it holds up to the abuse of wallets or back pockets. That being said, there are endless alternatives to standard card stock. Experiment with different materials that can be run through your printer or copy machine. Think about color, pattern, texture, and weight. A beautiful or surprising material becomes part of the content and imagery of your project. Keep your eyes open, and you'll find that just about anything can be transformed into a card.

METHODS When deciding whether to print, stamp, stencil, or write your content, remember that you'll need more then just one card, so use a method that is easy to produce in multiples. Use resources that are affordable and convenient as well as visually effective: if your neighbor runs a letterpress shop, by all means, knock on his door.

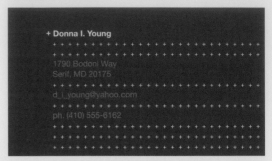

DESKTOP PRINTING Printing cards on your home printer is fast, easy, and cheap. Perforated card stock is available at most office supply stores, and usually includes instructions or software for formatting your file to fit the paper's layout. Vellum, transparency film, magnets, stickers, iron-ons, and fabric are just some of the alternate products you can buy. These are made specifically for either inkjet or laser printers, so choose with care.

Printing on found and homemade objects, such as magazine pages, subway fare cards, posters, or handmade papers, can yield exciting results. Some of these materials could damage your printer, so be careful; sandpaper, for example, is definitely not recommended.

HANDWRITTEN Sometimes you just need a card...FAST. What better way to expedite the process and simultaneously express yourself than to do-it-yourself? Cut paper (any will do, though something heavy is preferred) to size, add your relevant information, and Voila! Faster than you can say "Holla back!" you're ready to meet and greet.

LETTERPRESS Letterpress, the oldest form of typography, is expensive and time consuming, so design carefully and don't change your address anytime soon. The end result can be quite elegant, and worth the extra effort. Curved or angled text is difficult to set in hand-set metal type, but can be done from digital files. Vendors that specialize in wedding invitations and other short-run projects often provide letterpress services.

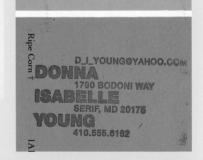

RUBBER STAMP Custom rubber stamp manufacturers can be found through most office supply stores. Provide your vendor with a high-resolution printout of your design to make the stamp. Thin lines and delicate details do not reproduce well, so stick with bold images and strong letterforms.

UNCONVENTIONAL Want to push the limits? Want your card to be unforgettable? Think outside all of the boxes and try these on for size. What better way to grow your business and satisfy a sweet tooth than with a brownie card? Or, express your inner termite with wood? Whichever way you go, go for broke and start networking!

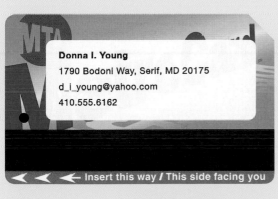

Todd St. John, of Hunter Gatherer in New York City, uses this method to design his business cards.

CD and DVD packaging

George Moore and Adam Palmer

CDs and DVDs are versatile, portable, affordable, and virtually unavoidable. Are you making your garage band's first EP? An interactive digital portfolio? A corporate safety training video? Whether your project aims to fit on a store shelf or stand out from the masses, a little thought and effort can deliver an innovative approach to how the package looks and feels, transforming a generic disk into a memorable physical object. Depending on the scale and budget of your project, you can apply your own style to mass-produced cases and labeling systems, or build original packaging from the ground up.

JEWEL CASE The easiest way to personalize your CD packaging is to make your own inserts for a plastic jewel case. Most computer graphics and layout applications feature templates with the proper dimensions for the standard jewel case booklet, tray card, and CD face. You can buy CD labeling kits that include perforated paper for tray card inserts and adhesive labels for the CD face. Alternatively, you can make a tray insert by printing your design onto any kind of paper and then cutting it down to size. Before folding, score the paper by running the rounded edge of paperclip (or a bookbinder's bone folder) against a ruler along the fold line.

There are several mass-produced alternatives to the standard jewel case that can add character to your package. Any container will have functional and aesthetic advantages (and disadvantages). A slimline jewel case, for example, takes up less space than a regular case, but it allows for fewer graphics. A clear clamshell case or an envelope with a window lets you put your graphics on the face of the CD itself.

SLIMLINE JEWEL CASE
The graphics printed on your CD can show through the case and become the cover, too.

CD PACKAGING OPTIONS Don't go the normal route. Experiment with different packages that fit the aim and scale of your CD project.

Our fictional band, Black Rainbow, needs to send out their demo CD to fifty venues and radio stations. The singer, Shane, wants to get these out as quickly as possible and deal with a full-on package later.

CARDSTOCK ENVELOPE
The best no-frills package is a cardstock envelope, available online at specialty disc packaging stores. You can customize it by adhering printed designs, wrapping it in some other patterned paper, applying stickers, or printing directly on the envelope. Also, consider adding another layer of packaging around the envelope, such as a plastic sleeve or a bubble envelope.

D.I.Y. DIGI-PACK

Make your own digi-pack. They look and feel so different from jewel cases but cost more to get manufactured. If you only need to make a few, make them yourself. Recycle the tray from a slimline jewel case and attach it to a card stock cover with a design of your own.

Janet plays guitar for Black Rainbow. She wants to put together ten CDs of the band's most recent recordings to send out to her ten favorite indie labels. She hopes the music will get noticed and figures that cool packaging will help.

Dirk, Black Rainbow's drummer, wants CDs to sell at the band's shows. The plan is to make them all the same but to make no more than fifteen at a time. He doesn't want to have too many extra CDs lying around after the full-length album comes out.

PHOTOCOPY WITH PLASTIC SLEEVE

Photocopiers provide fast, easy black-and-white reproduction. You can place three-dimensional objects on the glass, and the copier will make them flat. Set up your design on the computer, or be punk rock about it and use masking tape, cut-out letters, and markers.

LABELLING THE CD FACE goes a long way to creating the personality of your product.

BLANKS

• *Branded CD-R and DVD-R discs have the manufacturer's labeling already on them. In addition to being ugly, this branding is not your design, and it can show through your adhesive labels.*

• *Unbranded disks have a blank silver face.*

• *Printable discs are blank white or silver and can be printed on by some consumer inkjet printers (Epson r300 and r200).*

• *Screen printed discs can be ordered in bulk from some disk manufacturers. Then, you can burn them with your own data. Create a flexible design that you can use for several projects.*

HAND DRAWN
Draw directly on the surface with Sharpies or paint markers. Be careful not to scratch the surface of the disk. The top side of the disk where you are drawing is thinner than the read side.

SCREEN-PRINTED LABEL
Screen printing can be done by hand or commercially. It provides a clean, sharp look with simple graphics and line art. Photorealistic images and gradients don't translate well to the screen printing process. Bulk CD manufacturers use either UV curable screen printing inks or some form of thermal transfer.

CD LABELS

• Matte or glossy, the paper quality and finish make a big difference in the final product. Glossy labels have a more commercial feel, and the color appears brighter.

• An application tool keeps the label centered and smooth. Buy a starter kit that comes with a tool and a few paper options so that you can test which one suits your project.

PRINT ON CD

Some printers can accept printable CDs. Printing directly bypasses the need for adhesive labels that add thickness and cause balance problems if not centered. Check to see if you or any of your friends have a printer that prints onto CDs. Offer them an ink cartridge or a beer for the trouble.

ADHESIVE LABELS

Print or draw directly on precut adhesive labels before applying them.

Shane's friend Jeannie has been videotaping Black Rainbow's shows. They want to send out DVDs to some record labels. How better to explain the chaotic gentleness of a Black Rainbow set than to see it? They want to send out thirty DVDs, and it would be nice to have twenty more to sell at shows.

DVD CASE

If you want people to know that your disk holds video, put it in video packaging. DVD cases come in clear plastic and a variety of colors. Put your own design on the cover under the plastic sheet to make your project look polished and personalized.

FLOPPY DISK CASE

Go retro. Find those extinct floppy disks from your parents' attic and turn them into disk sleeves. A disk fits inside of the standard floppy sleeve perfectly. Make your own label or use the adhesive ones that came with blanks back in the 1980s.

Dirk and Shane were scavenging around in their apartment and discovered a stack of old floppies. Turns out they are about the same size as a CD. Shane kept searching and found some junk CD mailers. Voila! More instant CD packaging.

ISP CASE

Don't know what to do with all those internet service provider disks that keep clogging your mailbox? Throw the disk out and keep the sturdy cases they come in! Give them new life by covering them with maps or loading them up with stickers.

ZIG ZAG SHIRT
Design: Zvezdana Rogic
Photography: Nancy Froehlich
Model: Kate Taylor

Embroidery

Zvezdana Rogic

The age-old craft of embroidery has entered the machine age, populating our lives with corporate logos, monograms, and uniform badges. With the advent of customization, machine embroidery is now widely available as a stylish way of applying graphics to fashion. Make a brand for your family, your band, your circle of friends, or another social group. Fun, catchy images and symbols can turn the most mundane piece of clothing into a fashion statement. Create a cool design, have it embroidered, and go public!

HOW TO Machine embroidery vendors are easy to find online as well as in most business districts. You will pay a small set-up fee in addition to the cost per unit, which goes down as the quantity of pieces increases. Many vendors can also provide inexpensive shirts, jackets, caps, and bags.

Embroidered logos are typically found on breast pockets, cuffs, and baseball caps. While some vendors are sticklers for standards, others are friendlier to artistic invention and will accept more unusual orders.

• *Outline art takes less time to embroider than solid shapes.*

• *Create your art in black and white, without gray tones, and save as JPEG files. Most commercial vendors accept files on disk or paper printouts.*

• *Embroidery is a low-resolution medium. Save files at the size you would like your design to appear, at about 150 pixels per inch.*

• *Most machines can embroider no larger than 6 x 8 inches. Multi-color designs require more time and are thus more costly.*

• *Provide your vendor with a paper proof of your graphic at the exact size that it will be reproduced. Always ask to see an embroidered sample before having your whole job done.*

• *A digital embroidery machine, such as the Bernina, comes with a PC software program used to convert JPEG files to embroidery-ready stitch files. Downloaded to the embroidery module of the sewing machine, the file dictates the needle motion.*

SATIN STITCH
This long stitch spans the width of a shape. While it looks elegant, it is inappropriate for broad areas, since long threads tend to separate.

STEP STITCH
Used to fill an area with small, rapid stitches, this is the right choice for solid parts of your design.

OUTLINE STITCH
This stitch is used to outline the shapes in your design. Although this is often only the first step in embroidery, in some cases it makes an effective result by itself.

While most machines have automatic choice settings, you can also manually select the type of stitch that best fits your fabric and design.

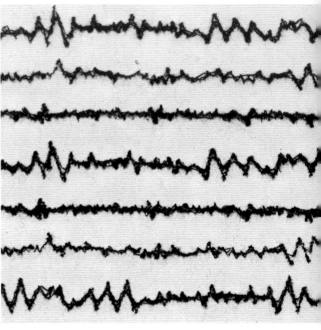

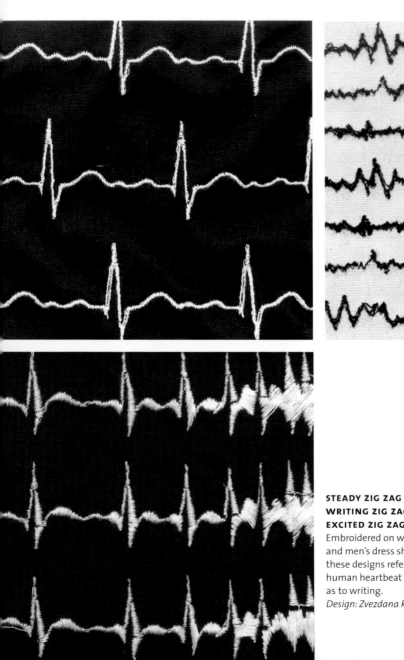

STEADY ZIG ZAG
WRITING ZIG ZAG
EXCITED ZIG ZAG
Embroidered on women's
and men's dress shirts,
these designs refer to a
human heartbeat as well
as to writing.
Design: Zvezdana Rogic

FREUDIAN SLIP
Design: Zvezdana Rogic

COMMA PATCH
Design: Spence Holman

COUNTRIES
Design: Zvezdana Rogic

I SCREAM GIRL
*Design: Zvezdana Rogic and
Nancy Froehlich*

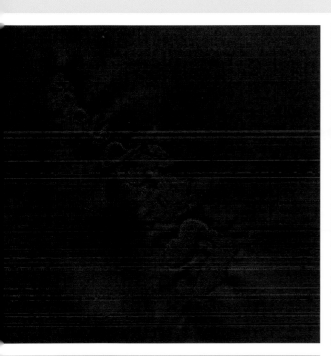

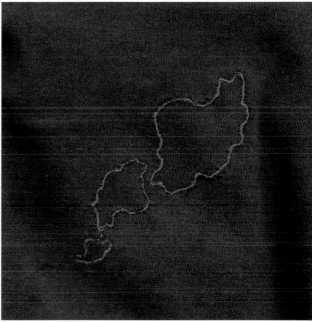

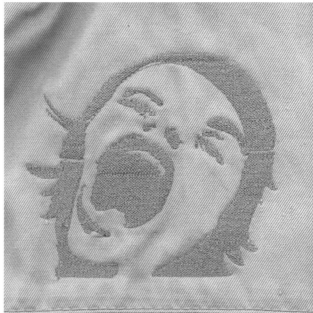

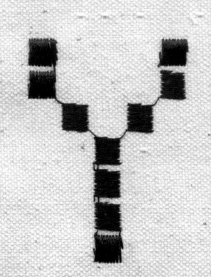

TROUBLED BIRD
MOMMA & DAD
This one-of-a-kind ornamental cuff was embroidered on a Bernina 180 machine.
Design: Melanie Freebairn

D.I.Y.
Logos are commonly embroidered on hats, shirts, and aprons as an alternative to screen printing. Here, we experiemented with embroidery on canvas and cardboard.
Design: Zvezdana Rogic

BUTTERFLY SHIRT
(opposite)
Design: Zvezdana Rogic
Model: Nancy Froehlich

Wms. Bros. Marketing
Sam & Ben Williams
Suite 1003
122 E Harry St.
Wichita Kansas 67211

RETURN TO SENDER
Looks alone won't get these
envelopes where they need
to go.

Use the following makeover
tips at right (courtesy of the
US Postal Service) to achieve
maximum mail satisfaction.

Envelopes

J. Spence Holman

Who writes letters anymore? The mail is great for magazines (the ones you don't borrow or read online, anyway), but it has been mostly relegated to the sad duty of delivering bills, credit card solicitations, and court orders. But it's a happier story when you receive that killer invitation to the local motorcycle fundraiser, get a birthday check from Grandma, or find your Radio Orphan Annie decoder pin in the mailbox. None of this would be possible without the humble envelope.

THE BASICS The envelope as we know it appeared around the seventeenth century. It has since evolved from a piece of paper cut and folded around a message to a piece of paper cut into a standard size, folded, and glued around a message. Paying attention to this standard is what ensures that your message gets where you want it to go.

If you ever have specific questions about your mail, the United States Postal Service's Web site, www.usps.com, is an exhaustive resource for all things sendable.

SIZE AND SHAPE Envelopes come in many sizes and shapes, but this doesn't mean that you should use all of them, or that the post office will mail them. In fact, with the exception of some emergency holiday situations, standard sizes should meet most of your needs.

The Postal Service officially defines a letter as being from 5 to 11 1/2 inches long by 3 1/2 to 6 1/8 inches high, no more than 1/4 inch thick, and one ounce or less. Anything bigger will require extra postage.

Regular envelopes that fit within these parameters can be found just about anywhere, and they are divided into series. Commercial envelopes are demarcated by numbers. One of the most common is the Number 10, which measures 9 1/2 by 4 1/8 inches, and easily fits a folded 8 1/2 by 11 inch piece of paper.

The Baronial (or Bar) series is typically used for invitations and cards, and comes with a pointed flap. The A series (*A* for announcement), which has a square flap, comes in similar sizes and is used in similar situations.

ENVELOPE BASICS

- *The recipient's and the sender's return address should be parallel to the longest side of the envelope.*

- *Use either a P.O. Box or a street address, but not both.*

- *Keep the bottom right of the envelope clear, as the Postal Service applies a 5/8-inch-tall bar code there.*

- *Fifteen sheets of folded paper in an envelope equals approximately 1/4 inch.*

- *One ounce is around four sheets of paper in a Number 10 envelope*

- *Envelopes with rounded corners will get caught in the mail sorting machines.*

- *Square envelopes require extra postage because the sorting machines cannot determine which way the address reads.*

THE WINDOW

Give your letter a chance to see the world, and don't let the address hog the view. Fill the window with something interesting (instead of boring text), and give your friend a sneak preview of what's inside.

Dr. W. J. Weiss
Post and Beam Press
26 Gudger Street
Asheville NC 28801

THE NONVELOPE

This is great for flyers, newsletters, and other bulk mailings that do not require any formality. Fold your paper into thirds, add an address, and mail. Use tape or a sticker—not a staple—to hold the paper together so that it does not run afoul of the postal sorting machines.

TREY AND THE
ROMANTONES
114 RHODE STREET
CINCINNATI OH 45237

J. Grimaldi
28 Market Street
Des Moines IA 50317

IN THE CLEAR

Grab a plastic pouch from your parcel carrier of choice, and attach it to an interesting backing. Address whichever side you choose, and remember that due to its size, this envelope will require extra postage.

Envelope design:
J. Spence Holman

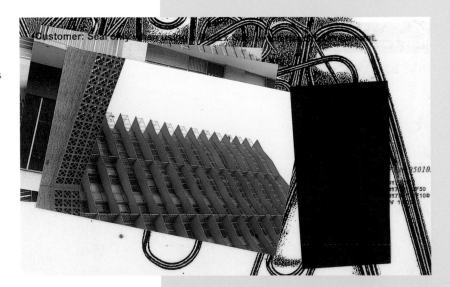

THE DECONSTRUCT

No one ever said your envelope had to be made of regular white paper. Take apart an envelope of any size and trace it onto interesting paper (Remember that the inside should be as interesting as the outside). Cut it out, fold it, and glue it together.

THE KNOCKOUT

Take scissors, an X-acto knife, or your trusty hole punch and make your own window pattern. Reveal a little or a lot. Are these holes in a construction fence, or just some interesting Swiss cheese? Be careful: too much perforation and your letter might not get past the doorstep.

Troy Roman
114 Rhode Street
Cincinnati OH 45237

LAURA BOYDSTON
43 GUTHRIE AVENUE
CLEVELAND OH 44102

INTER-DEPARTMENTAL ENVELOPE
Use Repeatedly Until All Spaces Are Utilized — Do Not Staple or Tape Flap

TO T. ROMAN
LOCATION 114 RHODE ST

TO CINCINNATT OH 45237

TO ERIC FRIEDMAN
LOCATION 1790 WATER ST.
SEATTLE WA 98178

THE READYMADE

Some envelopes are born interesting. Repurpose these for your own mailing pleasure.

Flyers

Alissa Faden

They wrap telephone poles, cover bulletin boards, and are forced into your hand on street corners. What makes you notice one, but ignore or trash the next? The next time a flyer actually attracts your attention, ask yourself what makes it eye-catching or noteworthy, so that you can create successful ads and announcements of your own. In these lost cat flyers, you'll find inspiration to create flyer designs to suit your own needs—whether that be scoring a purrfect roomie or selling the jeep you've had since you got your license. Now, go ahead and post some bills.

UNCOMMON COPY Flyers are commonplace, so make yours look different. A smart layout and bold graphics can provoke a double-take, while interesting text will seal the deal, drawing the viewer in for a closer look. Clever copy may eliminate the need for any picture at all. Play with puns, rhyming, and clichés. When your wording is nailed down, think about scale. Don't be afraid to make a word so huge it flows off the page. On the other hand, small, well-placed text can sometimes attract the eye better than big type, because the open space allows the eye to focus in.

REPRODUCTION If photocopying is your method of reproduction, embrace the look and feel of the medium. Copy centers generally have powerful machines that can deliver an intense and solid coat of black. Take advantage of this by creating the illusion of painting white on black paper. (The copier at your school or office may not be up to that kind of performance.) While reproducing your work in color will cost more, it can help your flyer stand out from the pack. If you can't afford color copies or prints, try copying in black on colored paper. Note: ink jet prints will wash off in the rain.

CAT GOT YOUR TONGUE?

• *Try using a rhyming dictionary to channel Dr. Seuss.*

• *Listen to your friends talk, and take inspiration from the slang they use.*

• *Make use of popular culture; put your own spin on recognizable lyrics and movie quotes.*

Flyer design: Alissa Faden
Photography: Nancy Froehlich

MY CAT IS A TYPICAL MALE

He's often lost and always too proud to ask for directions.

Samuel is a chubby tabby cat with green eyes and a scar on his tail. He's dressed to the nines in a red, white and gold plaid collar. If you find him hitting on you, and/or mooching off you please call 202-493-5309. Sammy can be a real pain, but I love him, and will do anything to have him back.

Men Seeking Felines

eyes, love the outdoors. Let's go play a game of cat and mouse. #2489

WHAT A CATCH tall male with short orange hair seeks loyal, intelligent house cat to share good times. You should be into cat nip and cat naps. #6006

WELL GROOMED SWM seeks reunion with purrrfect feline companion. We recently had a spat and she up and left with her tail between her legs. Her beautiful salt and pepper fur, and lean figure make her easy to spot. If you find her please call me at 881-8894.

TOTAL GENTLEMAN on the prowl for a lady, not a tramp. Me: suave, handsome and distinguished. Your: green

LOVABLE & EASYGOING DM with a house in Aspen and an apartment in NYC seeks pet that can deal with city life. I'll spoil you rotten by taking you to the park and buying you treats. #8893

SPONTANEOUS BM seeks LTR with nurturer. I'm ready to settle down and raise a litter of youngsters. #6007

GREEN-EYED TAURUS w/ dark hair. I may be stubborn, but fun to have cat fights with. I enjoy romantic walks and spending time in the sunshine. If you meet me, you won't be able to keep your paws to yourself. #6011

881-8894 881-8894 881-8894 881-8894 881-8894 881-8894 881-8894 881-8894

AN UNEXPECTED... Cat Call

where're you running off to pussycat?

Hey baby. I need help finding my kitty Telly. She is a leggy Siamese with short hair. She purrs loudly and is wearing a pretty pink bell on her collar.

Call **410-348-2349** if you find her to collect your $$$.

LOST

FUR IS MUCH DARKER ON LEFT FRONT LEG

PINK COLLAR WITH TAG READING "SOPHIA"

MUSCULAR AND SKINNY; CAN FIT IN SMALL SPACES

EAR IS WHITE AND HAS SCAR

BROWNISH ORANGE ABYSSINIAN

GENEROUS REWARD BEING OFFERED

CALL 8675309

got info?
SPILL

MISSING KITTEN

NAME: **bess**
HAIR COLOR: grey
AGE: **6 months**
DISTINGUISHING MARK: speckled p
LAST SEEN: 2/13/05
PHONE: 718-243-5354

DO YOU COPY?
Spend quality time coming up with your concept and wording, and the execution of your flyer will be a breeze.

Gifts

Michelle Brooks

Gift-giving is an expression of social bonds, a two-way exchange that serves both the giver and receiver. The more you give, the logic goes, the more you get. Making your own gifts can be an economical way to submit, with pleasure, to the spirit of giving while expressing your own interests and personality. The act of dressing a gift is also a chance for you to show your stuff. Gift wrapping can be economical and eco-conscious. Here are a few ideas for designing and wrapping original, personal gifts.

WRAPPING Aside from the satisfying sound of paper ripping, there is no reason to encase a gift under layers and layers of wrapping. Wrapping paper reveals a secret, but there are other ways to hide the big surprise. Design your own wrapping or look around for materials that can be recycled, decorated, or otherwise transformed.

REDUCE, RECYCLE, REUSE

• *Recycle newspapers, magazines, and shopping bags to use for wrapping.*

• *Recycle brown corrugated boxes. Use stickers and tape to cover unwanted printing.*

• *Look for boxes that can be altered to suit your gift. Express mailing boxes can be turned inside out and decorated.*

• *Be casual. Some gifts are good looking enough that wrapping can be used to decorate instead of hide.*

• *Start a soft-wrap revolution, and stop asking for gift boxes at the mall. A sweater hardly requires the industrial-strength protection provided by a printed card stock box. Or keep the box and decorate it with your own branding.*

• *Most sewing shops have brightly patterned quilting squares that are great for small gifts. Cinch them with yarn or ribbon or sew them into small gift bags.*

SWEET BOX
Empty candy or cookie tins can be made into gift boxes. Decorate them with stickers, markers, or paint. This pattern was printed on sticker paper (available at office supply stores).
Design: Michelle Brooks
Photography: Dan Meyers

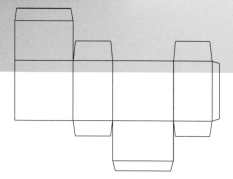

D.I.Y. BOX

Does it really need a ribbon? You can make a svelt little box that stands proud and bow-less.

Materials: printer, card stock, box for template, scissors or x-acto blade, double-stick tape, bone folder (for scoring)

1. Print your design on heavy weight paper (card stock).

2. Take apart a box that is the right size and shape.

3. Trace the outline of the box on the paper. Score the fold lines.

4. Cut and assemble.

Design: Michelle Brooks
Photography: Dan Meyers

STICKERS

Materials: labels, markers, pens or crayons
Design: Hannah Reinhard
Photography: Dan Meyers

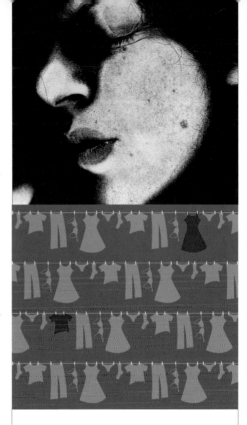

A sheet of 8 1/2 x 11 inch paper is the perfect fit for a CD. Use a scanner or copy machine to alter old Christmas paper. Design and print your own paper, or salvage discarded prints from your recycle bin. Put objects (or yourself) on the copy machine.

FROM YOURS TRULY
Design: Michelle Brooks, Nancy Froehlich, and Zvezdana Rogic

DELICATES
Pattern: Jessica Rodriguez

IT'S NOT A PAIR OF SHOES
Design: Michelle Brooks

PLAYCODE: CROSSHAIRS
Pattern: Kristen Spilman

8.5 in

11 in

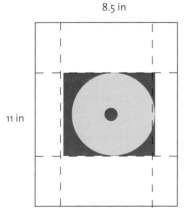

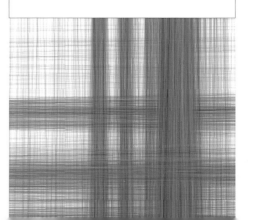

USABLE GIFTS Above all, you want to give a
gift that you would want yourself. Many of the
projects described in this book make effective
gifts (see BOOK, NOTE CARD, T-SHIRT, TOTE BAG).
Here are a few other handy applications for your
design skills.

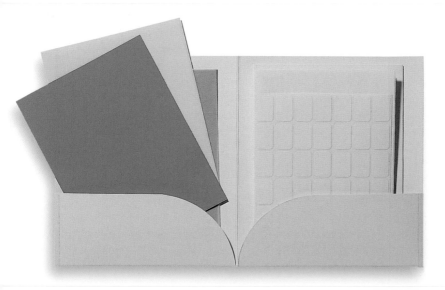

NOTEPAPER SET
Personally designed
notepaper makes an elegant
and dignified gift. This is also
a great gift for kids to give to
their teachers. Purchase blank
writing paper (complete
with box and envelopes), and
print the recipient's name
on each sheet in a suitable
font. For kids, put together a
folder with a few sheets of
interesting paper, envelopes,
and blank stickers that they
can personalize themselves.
Design: Michelle Brooks
Photography: Dan Meyers

HAMLET APRON

This apron is screen-printed with Shakespeare quotes about food and decay. Aprons can be purchased on the Web from uniform supply companies. Many are unisex and one-size-fits-all. You can print on aprons with the same processes used for t-shirts. Some suppliers also provide machine embroidery at a low cost, if you are producing a quantity of aprons.
Design: Ellen Lupton
Photography: Nancy Froehlich

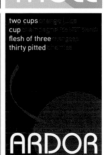

Adhesive-backed rubber magnets (business card size) are available from stationery stores and big-box office warehouses. They can easily be cut to a different proportion. For a children's gift, make a series of magnets that can be arranged into different characters. Let the kids color in the designs themselves. Laminate with packing tape.

ANTI-WAR MAGNETS
Design: Mike Weikert

PRINCESS MAGNETS
Design: Ruby Jane Miller
Photography: Dan Meyers

SMOOTHIE MAGNETS
(set of four recipe magnets)
Design: Michelle Brooks

Housewares

Davina Grunstein and Ellen Lupton

The patterns and messages that appear on commercially printed napkins, pillows, carpets, and coasters are designed to evoke a particular lifestyle: gracious, casual, contemporary, whatever. This chapter was put together by two working mothers who decided to create products that reflect their own lifestyles, not an idealized commercial one. We sought to bring a sense of humor—and a touch of irony and reflection—to the domestic realm. Irony is hard to come by at Pottery Barn or IKEA; some things, you have to design yourself.

WRITE YOUR OWN MONOGRAM
We used a standard monogram to announce the function (and attitude) of these hand towels rather than assert a family seal. The towels were ordered on-line from a company that offers a huge range of lettering styles and thread colors.

DEBRANDED PRODUCTS
Your bathroom is probably the site of dozens of brand messages, most of them designed to compete for attention on the drugstore shelf, not to look good in your house. We peeled the labels off of ordinary products and replaced them with hand-lettered office dots.

Design: Ellen Lupton
Model: Davina Grunstein
Photography: Nancy Froehlich

CLOTH NAPKINS are gracious and elegant as well as economical and eco-friendly. The black and white napkin on the far left was printed with a stencil, fabric paint, and a small paint roller.

The black-and-red napkins were screen-printed by hand on restaurant-grade polyester napkins. You can also use iron-on transfer material to print on napkins, but be warned: transfer designs cannot be ironed after they are produced, and transfer material will not take to

polyester napkins, so you will have to enjoy your cotton napkins in an unpressed state after their first washing. (We advocate "aggressive folding" for cotton napkins.)

COASTERS Apply your own graphics to cork or recycled rubber coasters with stencils, silkscreen, rubber stamps, or pasted paper, or have coasters printed in bulk commercially. Express a point of view while protecting your furniture.

BULK ORDERS can be printed commercially on cork or heavy paperboard, or on richer materials such as stone or leather. Coasters make great gifts, wedding favors, and party invitations.

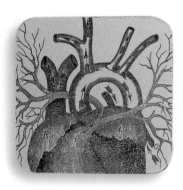

IRON-ON TRANSFER
You can buy blank white coasters on-line or at a craft store that are made from fabric-faced rubber (like a mouse pad). This material accepts the same iron-on transfer material used for t-shirts. Print your design onto the transfer material, flipped horizontally, and iron on. Reproduction quality is remarkably crisp (better than on a t-shirt).

RUBBER STAMP
Dip rubber stamps in paint for a rough and ready look.

Coaster designs: Ellen Lupton

CUT OR PASTED PAPER
Cut a circle from a laser print, a color copy, or a page from a book or magazine. Use the cut circles as disposable coasters, or laminate them and glue to a cork coaster. (Our design features flowers made from Prozac, Viagra, and other pills collected from e-mail spam.) Ink jet prints will bleed unless laminated.

NATURE MORTE PILLOW

Add your own layer of graphic commentary on top of an existing textile pattern. These pillows imprinted with flies and fetuses bring home the narrative of life and death.

There are various ways to apply graphics to fabric, including embroidery, fabric markers, fabric paints, and iron-on transfers. The pillows shown here were screen-printed by hand.

Design: Davina Grunstein
Painting: Dane Nester
Photography: Nancy Froehlich

Lisa's Dinner Party / Friday, September 8, 2006 / 6:00 pm / 250 Park Avenue / Dress to Impress / RSVP 410-828-6239

BBQ!

WE'RE GRILLING
OVER AT TOM'S PLACE

SATURDAY JUNE 4TH
12:00 NOON 'TIL WHENEVER

7021 HIGHFIELD ROAD
ALEXANDRIA, VIRGINIA

Invitations

Jessica P. Rodríguez and Ida Woldemichael

Whether you are planning a wedding, shower, benefit, or birthday party, an invitation is your first chance to make an impression on your guests. Use this opportunity to create intrigue, mystery, and excitement about the upcoming event while delivering all the necessary details in a concise and understandable way. Depending on your time, budget, skills, and the number of pieces you need to make, you can produce invitations by hand using desktop printing and a variety of found or purchased materials, or you can work with a commercial printing service.

DINNER PARTY VS. BBQ The style of your invitation should reflect the tone of your event. Will the party be relaxed and casual or formal and elegant? Will it include people from different backgrounds and generations (as in a wedding or a baby shower) or just your friends?

Your choice of imagery, typeface, colors, language, and materials will reinforce your message. The invitations to the left convey the elegance of a dinner party and the casual feel of a BBQ; in each one, the written information is integrated with the imagery.

POSTCARD INVITATIONS
Set the tone for your event with a simple postcard. Print it on your home or office printer, or have a large-scale job produced by an online postcard company, such as modernpostcard.com
Design: Ida Woldemichael Jessica Rodríguez

PLANNING YOUR INVITATION

- *What type of event will this be (birthday, wedding, graduation, baby shower, family reunion)?*
- *What is the age group (children, young adults, families, adults)?*
- *Will there be a theme (western, holiday, cocktail)?*
- *Is there a dress code (casual, semi-formal, formal, black tie)?*

- *What is the tone of the event (serious, humorous, relaxed, energetic)?*
- *What is your budget?*
- *How many invitations do you need?*
- *How much time do you have to make them before they need to be distributed?*
- *What are your output options (home printer, copy center, fax machine, e-mail)?*

CONTENT CHECKLIST

- *event*
- *time*
- *date*
- *location*
- *dress code*
- *RSVP*
- *contact information*

PARTY INVITATIONS You don't need to spend a lot of money to create interesting and fun invitations. Recycle, reuse, and repackage for low-budget but high-style invitations. Get ideas by looking around for materials and discovering new ways to use them. Give new life to interesting objects, paper scraps, old photos, containers, and packages that you might otherwise throw away.

ALTOID TIN INVITATION
Materials: Altoid tins, papers
1. Candy tins come in a variety of shapes and sizes. These are fun invitations to hand around at work or school.
2. Create a labeling system for the outside of the invitations. You can use sticker paper or a band of paper or ribbon with a guest's name on it. You can cover up the printing on the tin, or let it show.
3. Type or hand-letter the text, then print or photocopy.
4. Make confetti by cutting an accordian-folded strip of paper into narrow ribbons. Fill the box with confetti and lay the invitation on top.
Design: Ida Woldemichael
Photography: Dan Meyers

Don't open the can of worms! We're throwing a surprise party for Nate! Keep the confetti to throw on Nate!

Date: Saturday 01.28.06
Time: 7:00 pm
Place: 1500 Bolton St. #4
RSVP: Miriam 410.212.6981

party

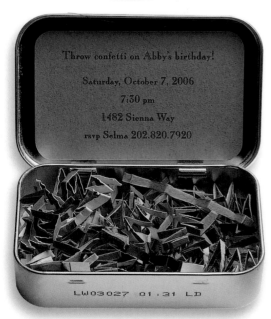

Throw confetti on Abby's birthday!

Saturday, October 7, 2006

7:30 pm

1482 Sienna Way

rsvp Selma 202.820.7920

LW03027 01:31 LD

To make confetti:

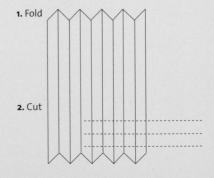

1. Fold

2. Cut

TEA-PARTY INVITATION

Materials: printable colored paper, glue, tea bag

1. Using a tea bag wrapper as a measuring guide, set up your dimensions in a layout program. Don't forget to leave an area for tabs that will be glued to close the sides of the tea bag.

2. Put address on the back of the tea bag or on an insert card. You can also place a message on the insert card like the ones shown above.

3. Close the tea bag with double-stick tape, and hand out your invitations.
Design: Ida Woldemichael
Photography: Dan Meyers

TEA-PARTY

SUNDAY, MARCH 5, 2006

1:00 PM

HILLARY'S HOUSE

500 MOSHER AVENUE

BALTIMORE, MD 21217

WEDDING INVITATIONS A wedding invitation may need additional pieces such as a map and directions to the event, a reply card and stamped reply envelope, bridal registry information, or special discount rates for hotel accommodations and airline group fares. Design all these elements to coordinate with each other. Some people hire a calligrapher to address the envelopes, but your own handwriting in wonderful ink can be just as nice. Don't forget to choose a great stamp.

TRANSLUCENT OVERLAY WEDDING INVITATION
Materials: decorative paper, translucent or medium-weight tracing paper, string or ribbon, hole puncher.
1. Research envelopes and decorative paper at a stationary, craft, or art supply store. Trim the decorative paper to desired size. (Consider the envelopes that you will use.)
2. Type or hand-letter your text in an area slightly smaller than the decorative card. Use guidelines or crop marks to make trimming easy. Print or photocopy the text onto translucent paper. Test the paper in your printer; the ink may need time to set and dry on this surface.
3. Trim the printed translucent page and place on top of the decorated sheet.
4. Punch two holes along the top edge of both papers simultaneously. Insert string or ribbon through the holes and tie into a bow.
Design: Jessica Rodríguez
Photography: Dan Meyers

THE PLEASURE OF YOUR COMPANY IS REQUESTED

AT THE WEDDING OF

Katie & John

SATURDAY THE TWENTY-FOURTH OF JUNE

TWO THOUSAND AND SIX

FIVE-THIRTY IN THE AFTERNOON

HUMICELLO GARDENS

SAN DIEGO, CALIFORNIA

R.S.V.P. BY JUNE 3
321-654-0987

In this design, the printed text of the invitation lays over a sheet of decorative paper, and the two sheets are tied together with a ribbon. Decorative papers and ribbons are available at craft stores.

Eritrean cross or other cultural symbol

couple's initials

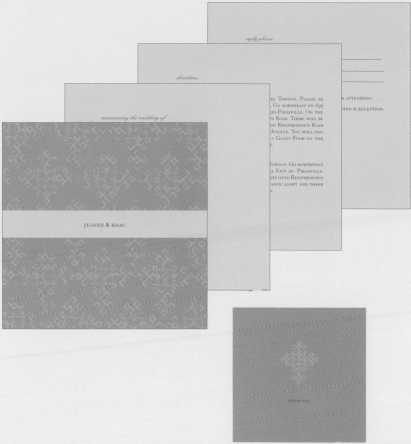

couple's initials and interlocking circles

BRAND YOUR WEDDING

1. Choose or construct a graphic symbol that is meaningful to the couple, such as interlocking circles, the couple's initials, an icon from a dictionary of symbols, or a religious mark.

2. Research paper and envelopes. The final invitation should be .25 inches smaller in both directions than the envelope. You can print the invitation on white or colored paper, or you can print a colored background,

as in the design shown here. The invitation can match or contrast with the envelopes.

3. Create a cover for your invitation with your symbol. Make a pattern by repeating the symbol, or use it by itself.

4. Apply your design to additional items such as a reply card and directions to the event. (The reply card will require its own envelope.)

5. Write and layout the content for the invitation and other inserts.

6. Print your invitation and

inserts back to back. (Test one before you print them all.) Trim as needed and fold in half to create a finished card.

7. For a small wedding (under fifty guests), this design is practical to print yourself on a desktop printer. For a larger event, consider having your design printed commercially.

8. You can apply your graphic symbol to other items needed for the wedding, such as programs, napkins, or thank-you cards.

Design. Idu Woldemichael

bride and groom stick figures

An icon can provide a look or "brand" that brings together the different parts of a wedding, from invitations to party favors and thank-you notes. The icon should reflect the couple: their profession, initials, humor, or culture.

TIE YOUR OWN KNOT

This wedding invitation plays with the vocabulary of do-it-yourself literature. The knots reappear throughout the various pieces, becoming an icon for the event.

The casual, homey tone of the invitation is offset by the formality of the hand-lettered envelopes.
Design: Jill Conrad and Christopher Hufnagel
Photography: Dan Meyers

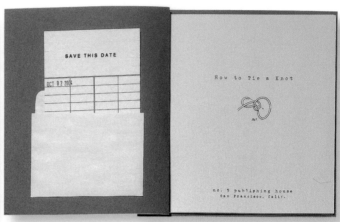

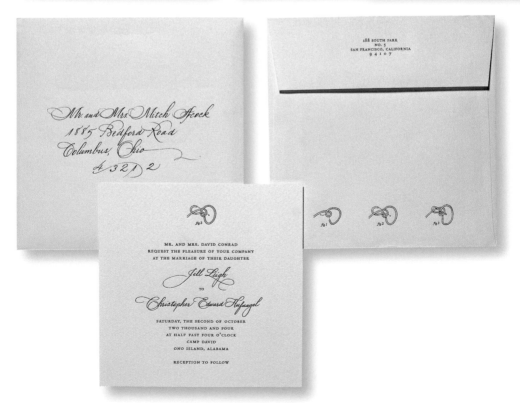

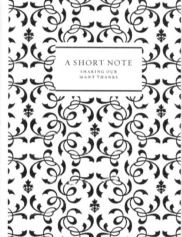

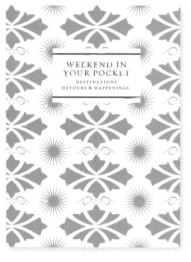

WEDDING IN YOUR POCKET

This wedding invitation was designed by a couple who have their own design studio in San Francisco. They created a series of tiny books that provided a useful guide for their guests and a wonderful way to remember the event. Each book is 3 1/4 x 4 1/2 inches, designed to fit into a purse or breast pocket. The whole series fits in to a hand-sewn linen sleeve.

Design: Becca Rees and Alex Ashton, Zipfly Design and Photography

Photography: Holly Stewart

Kids and design

Ellen and Julia Lupton

Kids are constantly assaulted with brand images and corporate cartoons, making the typical family birthday party a consumer-fest of licensed goods. Yet children are great artists and designers themselves. Encourage them to value their own creativity and help them put their personal mark on objects and media of their own design. Learn something new by making stickers, t-shirts, Web sites, and other stuff with your kids or your younger friends and siblings. Kid-designed products make great gifts for grandparents, and you might even want to keep some of these next-wave designs for yourself. As kids make their own stuff in response to their own publics, they will learn to navigate the shiny happy world of consumerism in a new way. Outfitted with the tools of taste, technology, and attitude, they just might make better choices for a better world.

GIRL POWER No need to be a fashion victim (or a Disney slave) when you can put your own fabulous drawings on a t-shirt. Use scissors to customize the fit of an ordinary shirt, and apply graphics using iron-on transfers, screen printing, or fabric markers. (See our T-SHIRT chapter for instructions and more ideas.) Younger kids will need assistance; teens can get going themselves and launch their own personal fashion lines.

T-SHIRTS
These screen-printed shirts feature original graphics by the next generation.
Design: Hannah Reinhard and Ruby Jane Miller
Production: Ellen Lupton
Models: Isobel Triggs and Ruby Jane Miller
Photography: Nancy Froehlich

FINALLY **5**

D.I.Y. CHARACTER DESIGN
Two eight-year-old girls got together and designed their own family of characters. Mom helped build a Web site, with biographies written by the kids.

The newly minted characters provided the theme for some younger siblings' birthday party, appearing on homegrown shirts, stickers, goody bags, and activity books.
Designers: Hannah Reinhard and Ronnie Hecht
Tech support:
Julia Reinhard Lupton

hanron–home1

.designwritingresearch.org/4-kidz/Spring-a-ling/   Q▾ Google

eBay   .Mac   Yahoo!   News ▾

SPRING-A-LINGS AND GLEN-O-DENS

http://www.desi

dh photo   Apple   Amazon   eBay

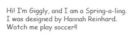

Hi! I'm Giggly, and I am a Spring-a-ling.
I was designed by Hannah Reinhard.
Watch me play soccer!!

My favorite color is green.

I like to listen to classical music.

My favorite thing to do is play soccer.

My favorite food is macaronii.

I am twelve years old.

SPRING-A-LINGS
AND
GLEN-O-DENS
AN ACTIVITY BOOK

BY
HANNAH
REINHARD
&
RONNIE
HECHT

THIS BOOK BELONGS TO

_____

BUILD YOUR OWN BRAND
Say good-bye to Hello
Kitty and apply your own
cool image to notebooks,
stationery, napkins, and more.
Design: Hannah Reinhard
Production: Ellen Lupton
Photography: Dan Meyers

BE A MEDIA SAVAGE
MediaSavage.com is the ever-evolving Web site of Jay Lupton Miller. His mom helped him build the site when he was nine, and he quickly learned to expand and maintain it on his own using Dreamweaver and Flash. Jay and his friends create short animated movies and post them on the site. Stick-figure animation (which has a vibrant subculture on the Web) provides an easy-access introduction to the art of animation. Kids and other beginners can create action-packed narratives without having Pixar-quality rendering skills.
Design: Jay Lupton Miller

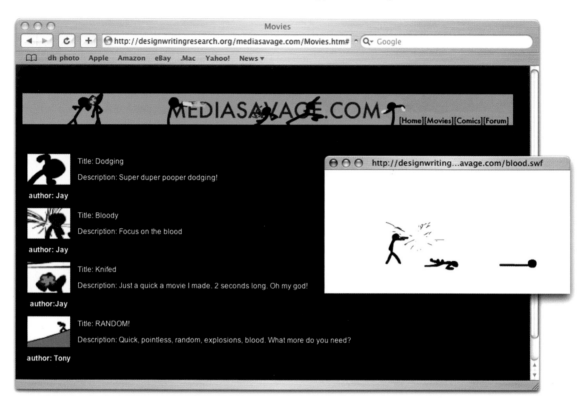

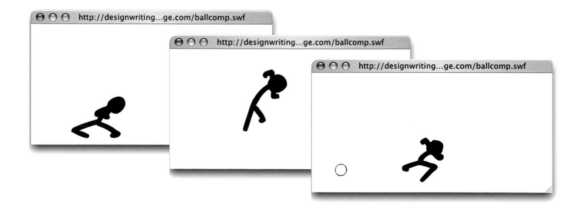

BAGS WITH A CUSTOM RING
Mom was eager to retire her
oversized Kate Spade tote.
She wanted a bag just big
enough for phone, cards,
keys, and cash. She ordered
small cotton bags on-line
(they cost a dollar each), and
commissioned her kids to
draw her phone in Sharpie.
She keeps a stock of blank
bags on hand, and when she
needs a new bag, presto, she
gets a new drawing.
*Design: Jay Lupton Miller
and Ruby Jane Miller for
Ellen Lupton*

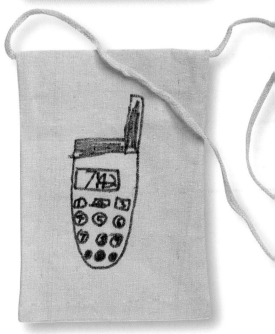

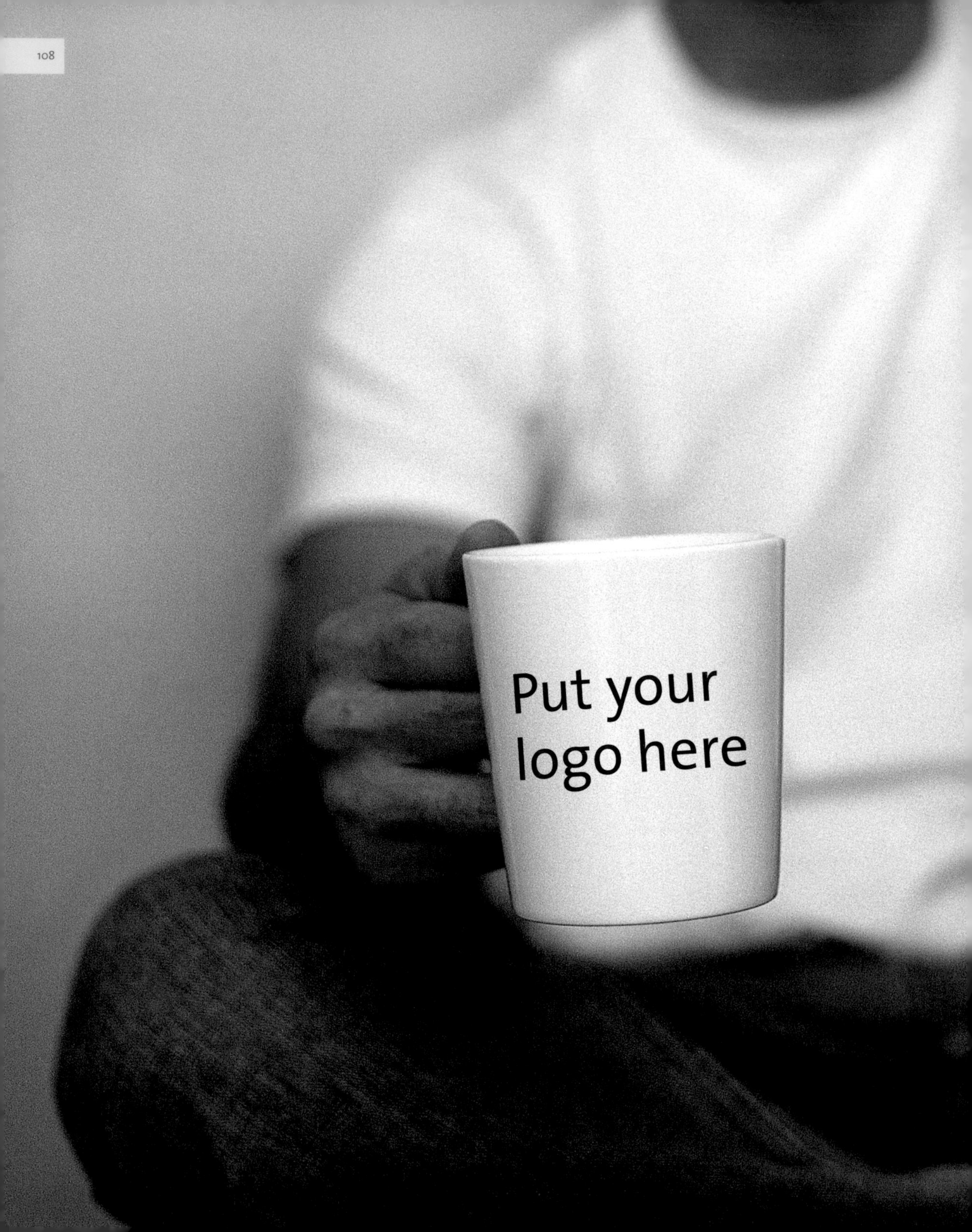
Put your
logo here

Logos

Mike Weikert

Picture your favorite T-shirt, the tattoo you got in high school, your fresh haircut, and the big green bowl you bought on eBay. These visual expressions help shape your identity—the way you present yourself and how others perceive you. Now, imagine taking these elements and distilling them into a single graphic representation that expresses your most distinctive characteristics. This distinctive mark would be your logo. You might put it on a business card, on labels for a product or CD, or on a T-shirt for your band, club, team or business.

PROCESS A logo is a graphic representation that identifies a company, product, or brand. Sometimes referred to as an emblem or mark, a logo can be typographic, pictorial or abstract. Logo design can be divided into three distinct steps:

1. RESEARCH AND IDEATION Analyze and define what you are trying to represent. Think, write, and sketch. Develop a list of attributes and characteristics that best represent your goals. Every thought and idea is relevant in this stage of the process.

2. DESIGN DEVELOPMENT Turn your ideas into form. Think of ways to visually represent the most important attributes using colors, symbols, and icons. Explore various fonts, and look for geometric and formal relationships using typography and individual letterforms.

3. FINAL EXECUTION Distill your ideas and forms into one clear concept. This is the stage for final revisions and reworking. Apply the final touches, and prepare your logo for the public eye.

RESEARCH AND IDEATION
"Going Public" is a fictional design event used as a case study for this chapter. Notice the relationships emerging from the letters in these concepual sketches.
All logo designs: Mike Weikert

LOGOTYPES Most logos include typography. The font chosen to represent your company, product, or organization plays a large part in determining the meaning and impact of your logo.

Many successful logos are simply typographic representations. This solution is known as the *logotype*, and it can stand alone or work together with *icons* or *symbols*.

DEVELOPING A LOGOTYPE

• *Type the name of your company, product, or organization in several different fonts. The personality and attitude change with each font.*

• *Experiment with serif, sans serif, and novelty typefaces. Think of the type as image.*

• *Choose a few directions that seem appropriate, and start combining type with icons or symbols.*

• *Try typing in uppercase and lowercase. Capital letters can make a mark look more serious or formal, while lowercase letters often feel more casual and relaxed.*

---

serif

going public
Minion Regular

going public
ITC New Baskerville Roman

going public
Didot Regular

going public
The Serif Plain

Going Public
Minion Bold

Going Public
ITC New Baskerville Bold

Going Public
Didot Bold

Going Public
The Serif Bold

going public
Edwardian Script

sans serif

going public   gp
Chalet Paris

going public   gp
VAG Rounded Light

going public   gp
Chalet Tokyo

Going Public   gp
Helvetica Neue Regular

Going Public   GP
Gotham Book

Going Public   GP
Berth. Akzidenz Grotesk Regular

GOING PUBLIC GP
Interstate Bold

GOING PUBLIC   GP
Trade Gothic Bold

GOING PUBLIC   GP
The Sans Semi Bold

novelty

GOING PUBLIC
Brooklyn Kid

GOING PUBLIC
Flyerfonts Reject

GOING PUBLIC
Warehouse

GOING PUBLIC
Stencil Bold

GOING PUBLIC
LCD Italic

GOING PUBLIC
Bubbledot

GOING PUBLIC
Fake Receipt

DESIGN DEVELOPMENT
Type studies and several design directions for a Going Public logo.

ICONS AND SYMBOLS An *icon* is an image that represents something based on resemblance, such as a graphic illustration of a man, woman, or dog.

A *symbol*, on the other hand, represents by association, but not necessarily by resemblance. A symbol can depict an idea that is abstract or has no physical form. The standard symbols for recycling and biohazard are both abstract.

DEVELOPING AN ICON

• *Try starting with icons and symbols that are recognizable, but add a personal twist for your company, logo, or group.*

• *Combine letterforms with graphic elements to create a unique logotype.*

• *There are many viable solutions when designing a logo. Don't be afraid to try several different directions.*

LOGO STANDARDS Think about how your logo will be used and create simple logo standards to avoid potential problems as your logo goes public. How many colors should be used for the primary logo? Does the logo work well in one-color? Can it be knocked out of a dark background? Is the logo legible at small sizes?

Designers create logo standards in order to provide clean art and simple guidelines for outside vendors such as printers and sign makers.

GOING PUBLIC LOGO STANDARDS

PRIMARY LOGO

Logo standards can be set up as vector art in Adobe Illustrator. That way, a digital file can be easily sent to vendors and printers.

Consider appropriate one-color applications as well as how the logo will look on a colored background.

ONE-COLOR OPTIONS

TWO-COLOR REVERSE-OUT OPTIONS

Test your logo at small sizes. A mark that is overly complex may not read well when shrunk down for a tiny newspaper ad or other application.

.75"

SMALLEST SIZE

FINAL EXECUTION
From T-shirts and Web sites
to buildings and vans, logo
applications are endless.
Plaster your logo everywhere
to give your company, product,
or group voice and visibility.

The Masthead

The masthead might include the logo or name of the group or business, a tagline that supports the group's identity, and, depending on the frequency of publishing, the publication date, volume, and issue numbers.

Headlines provide titles for articles and draw readers in.

You might use bigger, bolder type in the headline of your lead article, and smaller type for less important articles or regular departments. A headline can have two levels of information, such as a short, intriguing phrase followed by a second line of text (in a smaller or lighter font) that summarizes a point or provokes the reader to delve deeper.

THE LEAD ARTICLE could be the organization's mission statement, a letter from the editor, or a topical article.

BODY COPY is typically set in type ranging from 9 to 11 points; older readers or people with poor eyesight will prefer larger type (12 to 14 points). The smaller the type size, the more text will fit within a column.

SUBHEADS are used to break long articles into smaller sections. Subheads should be visually subordinate to the headline.

Pull quotes are provocative statements lifted out of the body of an article.

PULL QUOTES are enticing snippets that can be treated in a special font—perhaps italic, in a larger size than the body copy—that suggests interest but not necessarily importance.

SIDEBARS create visual variety on the page and allow you to present short pieces of information. You can set off a sidebar from other content on the page by drawing a box around it, putting a tone of color behind it, or using a different typeface.

ILLUSTRATIONS can make your pages more interesting and informative. Use photographs, clip art, or drawings by people from your readership. Even standard stock images can be used with wit and intelligence. Position pictures in relation to the content they support, and make the size appropriate to your goals. What will the picture mean to your readers? How does it illuminate the article?

Newsletters

Jessica P. Rodríguez

A newsletter is a small-scale newspaper that targets a specific audience. For example, residential communities publish articles about meetings, activities, and issues concerning their neighborhoods. A relevant newsletter begins with relevant content, so start by gathering the information you need from your various constituents and contributors. The editor (who may also be the designer, art director, photographer, and subscription manager) decides what information is most important, what headlines and subheads are needed, and how the content should be illustrated.

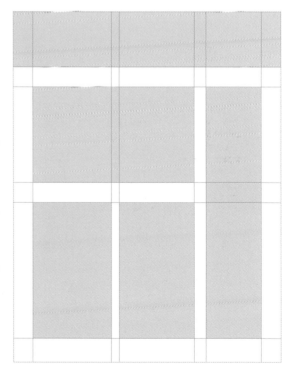

DISTRIBUTION A printed newsletter can be handed out at an event, left under doors, mailed inside an envelope, or mailed by itself. A self-mailed newsletter has room on one side for mailing information. If you decide to fold a letter-size newsletter in half (to 8 1/2 x 5 1/2 inches) for mailing, make sure the mailing panel remains visible on the outside. The folded piece can be held shut with a sticker or clear round seal (wafer seal). Permit numbers or a mailing indicia will be needed if the piece is being sent via a special class, such as bulkmail. For more information on mailing restrictions, visit The United States Postal Service Web site at www.usps.com/directmail.

THE GRID *is the architectural foundation of a newsletter—a set of non-printing lines that establish boundaries within a page. The vertical lines create spaces for columns of text, while the horizontal lines divide the page into additional zones. The grid also establishes the outer margins of the page.*

Swinging Seniors

modern living for active elders | June 2006

Grandma and Grandpa Out for a Date?! Heck yeah!

Dating is no longer reserved for those starting a family. Many of us mature people have already experienced what it's like to get married, buy our first home, and even watch our children be born and grow up into adulthood. Some of us have lived our lives to the fullest and completed every expectation we ever had about family life, and yet, for various reasons, we may find ourselves being single at an age when we are not expected to be dating. We feel young and energetic, and we look forward to many years of life ahead. It's time we take charge of our new future. Whether you're looking for a friend, a fling, or a life companion, there are multiple opportunities for social encounters.

Back to school.

How many times have you been interested in learning a new language, a new craft, or dance style, yet you never found the time to do so? Well, now is your big chance! There are classes offered all year round by community centers and adult education programs that cover everything from sculpture, guitar lessons, sushi rolling, tai chi, Italian, wood-working, salsa dancing, creative writing, and just about anything you could wish for. Taking a class (or teaching one) will connect you with people in your community that share your interests. Get to class a few minutes earlier, linger a little later after, and you strike up conversations that could develop into lasting friendships.

Roll up your sleeves.

With so many wonderful organizations in town, you are bound to find a volunteer opportunity that will make you feel better about yourself and introduce you to other caring individuals in your community. Are you good with numbers? Consider becoming a math tutor to a child. Do you like to build things? Try joining organizations that build or remodel housing for families in need. Do you knit in your spare time? You can donate knitted hats for newborn babies in hospitals or make blankets for the homeless. Whatever your interests are, you are bound to find an excellent match for a volunteer experience that will be filled with generous people just like you.

Lead the way.

If you enjoy a night at the theater or an afternoon at the local concert hall, consider a volunteer or part-time job as an usher. Your main responsibility is to greet patrons and show them the way to their seats. What better way to meet hundreds of people in a single day? And that's not all. In most venues, once the show begins, the ushers are allowed to stay for the duration of the event, so you'll get to see all your favorite shows for free!

Inbox is full.

If you like to maintain contact with family and friends over e-mail, try an online dating service. There are so many available these days, many of them tailored to certain interests, religious affiliations, and age groups. This is a great chance to meet a special friend or love interest. You can get to know several people at the same

ONE-COLOR NEWSLETTER ON PRE-PRINTED STOCK

• We designed the masthead to be printed in advance, in bulk, in a single color of ink, (spot color) allowing us to photocopy the newsletters onto this existing stock for each issue.

• A two-column grid allowed us to break down the content into chunks. Some elements cross over both columns.

• For the content of the newsletter, we used a single type family (Franklin Gothic) in a variety of weights and sizes. The subheads are shown in the same font used in the masthead. Establish a range of type sizes for your articles, headlines, and subheads.

• We used a relatively wide margin around the page to make it feel more generous. Always leave a margin of at least 1/2 inch to prevent content from getting cut off during output or reproduction.

SIMPLE The most basic newsletter is printed on letter-size paper (8 1/2 x 11 inches), using clean, simple text. Our sample design uses an interesting page format that editors could implement on their own, without help from a professional designer.

SPOT COLOR *Reproducing a photograph in full color requires four colors of ink (cyan, magenta, yellow, and black, the same colors used in an ink-jet printer). A cheaper alternative is to use a spot color, a unique ink color selected from a standard color system such as Pantone. You can use spot colors for illustrations and typographic elements to create a two-color newsletter.*

"I'll bring a date if you bring one, too."
Oh, the joys of group dating!

So you've had your eye on someone in particular, yet you don't quite feel ready to approach them one-on-one? I know! How about a group date!!

Strength in numbers.
Have you ever wished you had your best buddies backing you up and giving you their opinion during one of your dates? Well, your wish could come true! The best part of a group date is that the pressure is not all on you. You don't even need to have a specific person as a date. This is a

activities that can be done in a casual setting, where there's lots of open space and many opportunities for conversations among smaller groups of people. Consider going bowling. You don't need to be a rock star bowler in order to impress a special someone. This is all about having fun with a group of friends. So, lace up those fancy-shmancy shoes and warm up that arm! The great thing about a bowling group date is that there is plenty of down time for those waiting for their turn. This hanging out makes it a great opportunity for striking up

divide the food to be brought, so you can all contribute something without breaking your wallets, and you'll have a chance to enjoy great music, great weather, and even greater connections with friends. You can initiate a conversation with an interesting someone by simply offering some of the food you brought or asking about the great recipe they contributed. Simple as that. Not feeling a love connection? Just excuse yourself with the idea of wanting to try another dish from the other side of the group, and you're free to move around.

JUNE 2006
VOLUME IV
ISSUE NO. 3

Swinging Seniors
MODERN LIVING FOR ACTIVE ELDERS

Grandma and Grandpa Out for a Date?! Heck yeah!

Dating is no longer reserved for those starting a family. Many of us mature people have already experienced what it's like to get married, buy our first home, and even watch our children be born and grow up into adulthood. Some of us have lived our lives to the fullest and completed every expectation we ever had about family life, and yet, for various reasons, we may find ourselves being single at an age when we are not expected to be dating. We feel young and energetic, and we look forward to many years of life ahead. It's time we take charge of our new future. Whether you're looking for a friend, a fling, or a life companion, there are multiple opportunities

strike up conversations that could develop into lasting friendships.

Roll up your sleeves.
With so many wonderful organizations in town, you are bound to find a volunteer opportunity that will make you feel better about yourself and introduce you to other caring individuals in your community. Are you good with numbers? Consider becoming a math tutor to a child. Do you like to build things? Try joining organizations that build or remodel housing for families in need. Do you knit in your spare time? You can donate knitted hats for newborn babies in hospitals or make blankets

continued on next page

Start Rehearsing...
Open Mic Night is Back!

Let's bring our razzle and dazzle out into the spotlight! If you like to perform (you know who you are…), come on out and share the fun with your neighbors. A sign-up sheet will be posted on the entrance door of our building starting next week. You will find five different performance categories: singing, dancing, playing a musical instrument, stand-up comedy, poetry reading. Sign your name under the category (or categories if you're an over-achiever), and let the rehearsals begin. You can participate as an individual or as an ensemble—if you're a singer, gather up friendly neighbors to be your backup singers, dancers, and musicians. You get the idea: the more the merrier. Performance night will be Friday, June 23rd, starting at 7:00 p.m. in our first floor Lounge. Special prizes will be awarded for each category, in addition to a best performance award. For those of you who haven't yet warmed up to the idea of performing this time around, come cheer your neighbors and enjoy a night of free entertainment!

Eat outside.
As soon as the weather warms up, chairs and tables come out onto the sidewalks from local restaurants and cafés. This is a great way to enjoy some people-watching. If the idea of dining out by yourself intimidates you, try it outside. You won't have to stare at your food the entire time, since there will be plenty to look at. Not only could you bump into someone you know walking down the sidewalk, but you could also strike a conversation with diners at nearby tables who tend to be more willing to socialize with strangers when outdoors. While you check out people, you allow others to check you out as well. Sip with a saucy or intriguing title on the cover, and you might just bump into someone with a shared curiosity.

Rekindle an old flame.
Has it really been that many years? Look up alumni organizations from your former high school or college. They organize regular events for graduates, and your particular class may get together every few years. You may just bump into a former crush or meet someone you never quite noticed before. You will both have a common ground to start up conversation, reminiscing about the good ol' days and swapping memories about campus life.

Whatever your style may be, there are numerous ways to begin expanding your social circle. Be creative and you will not only enjoy yourself but you will very likely meet interesting new people.

There's a Reason Why It's Called
WORKING Out

Exercising might not be at the top of your favorites list, but you know it's good for you, and there are many options you can try in order to find one that you'll enjoy. You do not have to spend an hour jumping in front of your tele-vision to follow an exercise video; you don't have to run five miles on a track, and you certainly don't need to spend lots of money on a gym membership. Did you know that our fitness room, located on the

The best exercise will be the one you enjoy and to which you will remain loyal.

basement of our building, is stocked with the latest fitness equipment on today's market? Our very own personal trainer can design an exercise regimen for your personal goals and limitations. Don't let the machines intimidate you. Brenda will explain in detail how to adjust them to fit your body, and she is present at all times to insure your safety while exercising. Does walking on a treadmill bore you? Why not try one of our weekly fitness classes? Daisy, our fitness

instructor, leads the way every weekday on a variety of group classes that are open to all fitness levels. For more infor-mation on the fitness room class schedules and hours of operation, see the sidebar on the right.

Still not convinced about visiting the fitness room? Don't let that be an excuse to skip on exercising. There are many things you can do to keep your body healthy. Do you enjoy taking walks? Grab a friend and take a brisk walk for at least a half hour to get your heart moving at a higher rate. If it's raining out, move your walk to the nearest shopping mall and walk while you look at the store windows (now, don't go stopping at every store!). Want more challenge? Skip on taking the elevator to your floor and try the emergency stairs instead. Not interested in breaking a sweat? Try gardening, cleaning your car, or even acting as a volunteer at a local soup kitchen, or any other activity that will keep your body in motion for an extended period of time. The best exercise will be the one you enjoy and to which you will remain loyal. Be consistent, and remember that even a little bit of exercise is much better than a whole lot of nothing.

FITNESS ROOM
Class Schedule and Hours of Operation

MONDAY
Fitness room hours:
7:00 a.m. – 9:00 p.m.
Cycling class:
8:00 a.m. – 9:00 a.m.

TUESDAY
Fitness room hours:
7:00 a.m. – 9:00 p.m.
Step class:
8:00 a.m. – 9:00 a.m.

WEDNESDAY
Fitness room hours:
7:00 a.m. – 9:00 p.m.
Cycling class:
8:00 a.m. – 9:00 a.m.

THURSDAY
Fitness room hours:
7:00 a.m. – 9:00 p.m.
Step class:
8:00 a.m. – 9:00 a.m.

FRIDAY
Fitness room hours:
7:00 a.m. – 3:00 p.m.

SATURDAY
Fitness room hours:
7:00 a.m. – 11:00 a.m.

SUNDAY
Fitness room hours:
7:00 a.m. – 11:00 a.m.

Lead the way.
If you enjoy a night at the theater or an afternoon at the local concert hall, consider a volunteer as part-time usher as an usher. If you can read, you will be qualified for the job. Your main responsibility is to greet patrons and show them the way to their seats. What better way to meet hundreds of people in one single day? And that's not all. In most venues, once the show begins, the ushers are allowed to stay for the duration of the event, so you'll get to see all your favorite shows for free!

Inbox is full.
If you like to maintain contact with family and friends over e-mail, try an online dating service. There are so many available these days, many of them tailored to certain interests, religious affiliations, and age groups. This is a great chance to meet a special friend or love interest. You can get to know several people at the same time without making any early commitments or hurting anyone's feelings. Once you feel you've met a person that shares a special connection with you, you can schedule a meeting in a public place where you can reintroduce yourselves and safely interact in person.

SOMEWHAT SIMPLE A more elaborate newsletter might be printed on tabloid-size paper (11 x 17 inches). Folded in half, a tabloid sheet becomes a letter-size document with four pages. The newsletter shown here adds illustrations to the basic typographic mix, and it utilizes a second color (spot color) throughout the design.

TWO-COLOR NEWSLETTER

• This design uses black ink for text and a spot color for titles, subheads, and illustrations.

• The illustration is printed in two different percentages of orange, our spot color. As the color becomes lighter, we can overlap text on top of the illustration without compromising legibility.

• The three-column grid allows sidebars and boxes to extend both vertically and horizontally.

• If your printing budget allows you to use a trimmed sheet of paper instead of a pre-cut sheet, then you can extend some of your artwork beyond the edge of the page. This is called a bleed. Use bleeds to create a sense of scale and dynamism. Text areas should still stay a safe distance from the edge.

ALL OUT This newsletter features full-color photography, which means the piece will be reproduced by a commercial offset printing company in four colors (cyan, magenta, yellow, and black). Although newsletters can be created in any page size, we have followed the dimensions used on our previous example: a tabloid sheet (11 x 17 inches), folded in half to create a four-page, letter-size document. This all-out newsletter, however, will be eight pages instead of four, so we will have to set up the files as *printer spreads* (see opposite page).

ELECTRONIC NEWSLETTER

- *The typography of an electronic newsletter will need to reflect the selection of fonts you can expect end-users to have on their own computers. (See WEB chapter.) Our design uses plain-vanilla HTML for the main text and headings; the masthead is a GIF image.*

- *The width of your page should accommodate a range of screen monitors. Ideally, you should be able to see the entire width of an electronic document at once.*

- *It's advisable to work with a one- or two-column grid in the limited space of an e-newsletter.*

- *You can make one long page that scrolls vertically, or you can create multiple short pages connected by links.*

- *The list of articles (table of contents) could work as either anchor links within*

the same page or as links to other pages.

- *Since an electronic newsletter will be viewed on a computer screen, the colors must be in RGB mode. Images must be saved in JPEG or GIF formats at 72 dpi.*

GOING "E" The most cost-efficient newsletter is an electronic one. You have no printing and paper costs, and your distribution can be basically free of charge, since the newsletter is sent like e-mail. (Be mindful of anti-spam laws, though.) To design this newsletter, you will need to consider the same concepts guiding printed publications along with the special restrictions of Web design.

PRINTER SPREADS EXPLAINED

In order to bind together two folded sheets to make an eight-page document, the pages must be assembled in a special order. The front cover (or page one) is printed to the right side of the last page (page eight), so that when the final publication is folded, the cover ends up

on the front, and page eight ends up on the back. In any multi-page publication, the number of pages must be divisible by four. Commercial offset printing firms will generally do this step for you, but it is important for any D.I.Y. designer to know what is involved.

first sheet		second sheet	
8	1	6	3
2	7	4	5

Note cards

Ida Woldemichael

A note card is a flat or folded card with no pre-printed greeting. You can make your own note cards with simple materials and techniques. Use personal imagery such as digital photographs, or invent your own decorative patterns. After all, you know your subject better than Hallmark. Note cards are worth keeping, they never get dated, and they can fit almost any occasion. The inspiration for a great design may be right in your home.

A SET OF NOTE CARDS makes a great gift. The cards in a set can have the same design and colors, or they can include a variety of designs in coordinating or contrasting colors. Individual cards can be cut out of a larger pattern. Design your own pattern or use vintage wallpaper, wrapping paper, or fabric. To package a set of note cards, make a belly band from paper to hold the set together, or put them in a box or clear cellophane envelope.

PHOTO CARDS

1. Print a background design and message for your card. The card above is screen-printed.

2. Create a clipping path of your favorite digital or scanned photo.

3. Print the photo on sticker paper, trim, and adhere to the card.

Design: Ida Woldemichael

OBJECT INSPIRED CARDS

Even food has an interesting design. The pattern on this card is inspired by ramen noodles. Be inspired by foods with interesting shapes like macaroni, rice, or cheese.

PATTERNED CARDS

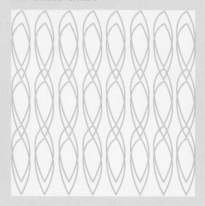

A simple almond shape was used to create this pattern. The shape is repeated vertically and arranged in a staggered pattern. You can try this with many different shapes.

TYPOGRAPHIC CARDS

A game can make a fun design. This card uses a hidden word game to say "happy birthday." Use a bold color to make your message stand out. You can also circle or strike through your message.
Design: Ida Woldemichael

COLORED PAPER CARDS

Materials: colored paper, printed paper, decorative brads or other hardware (optional), adhesive or double-sided tape

1. Trim a sheet of colored paper to desired size. Fold in half to create a card.

2. Cut a narrow strip of printed paper to the same length or width as the folded card, or a square, or any other shape.

3. Attach the printed paper strip onto front cover of your card with adhesive or double-sided tape, or print your own design on adhesive-backed label paper. You can use decorative brads or other hardware to emphasize the constructed quality of the card.
Design: Jessica Rodríguez
Photography: Dan Meyers
Cartoon detail: Chris Ware

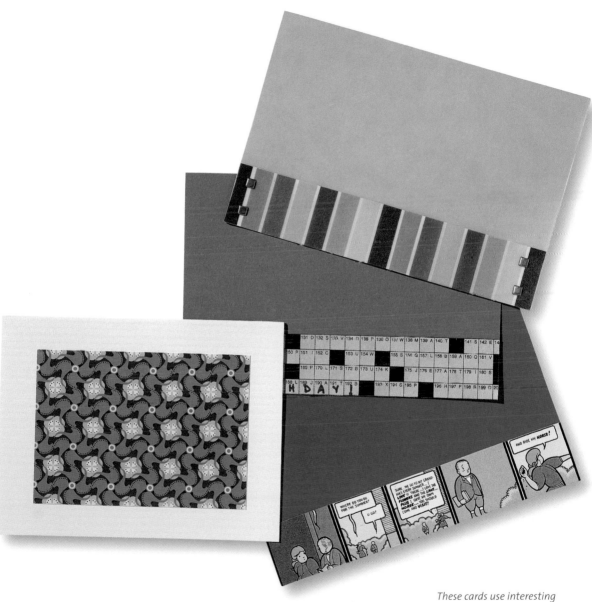

These cards use interesting combinations of colored and decorative paper. You can purchase paper at a craft store, find materials around your house or office, or paint or print your own patterns.

Photo albums

Julia Lupton and Jennifer Williams

Behind every photo album is an ego—yours. But inside that ego lives an historian, an artist, and a philosopher. The historian is recording, editing, and preserving the past. The artist is arranging and embellishing pictures on the page. And the philosopher is thinking about the ideas that illuminate all this stuff. Whether it's love or fortune, self or sociability, the passage of time or its glorious denial, civilization or its discontents, somewhere in every album an idea is struggling to be put into words and pictures. If you recognize and embrace the passion and purpose behind each act of cutting and pasting, your albums will be smart, sharp, and beautiful.

SCRAPBOOKING has gone public. A vast array of specialized tools and fancy materials, as well as books, zines, and Web sites, have emerged to build (and profit from) this popular hobby. Home-based workshops, run by entrepreneurial housewives on the Tupperware model, provide training and idea exchange—along with the inevitable consumer opportunity. Although most albums document family events, some practitioners are using scrap-books to promote their small businesses (such as dental offices and home daycare centers). Other scrapbookers start their own businesses in order to develop quirkier supplies than those promoted by the big companies. The Internet allows one-of-a-kind books to be displayed, furthering the public dissemination of these once-private documents.

You can make personal and original photo-graphic documents while avoiding the extra layers of vellum, lace, and buttons that drape the overdressed albums of today's scrapbooking scene. Off with the corset, on with the idea! If you really need your wedding album to look like a wedding cake, make your icing out of materials and images that you find yourself. Hey, it's a scrapbook—use real scraps, not fake ones that come in cellophane bags. As a graphic design project, the photo album can encompass everything from book-binding and photography to collage, writing, and typography. Identify your goals and your talents, and go ahead and make history.

SCRAPBOOK PHILOSOPHIES

• *The book's the thing:* instead of buying an album, recycle an old diary, almanac, atlas, comic book, recipe file, or binder. Its previous life provides background for the story you want to tell.

• *Have a point of view.* Are you thinking like a scientist or a poet? A journalist or a romantic? Find the ideas mixed in your memories, and bring them forward through thoughtful framing of your materials.

• *Ideas rock.* Add content, concept, and typography through scraps of text from poetry, old dictionaries, maps, or songs.

• *Be real.* Your own writing in your own hand is an authentic alternative to the prepackaged sentiments sold at craft stores.

• *Be an archaeologist.* Mix materials and memories from different times and places. Juxtapose and counterpoint the layers of your life.

PRESERVE

This photo album uses techniques from the "altered book" movement, the funky cousin of the more commercial Creative Memories industry. An abandoned lab notebook sets the tone for a loving yet clinical study of early childhood. Botanical illustrations meld contemporary science with Victorian natural history.

Scraps from an old French-English science dictionary spell out the scientific framework in the rhythm of elementary school. The mother's own handwriting provides an authentic voice of observation.

Design and baby photography:
Jennifer Williams
Book photography:
Dan Meyers

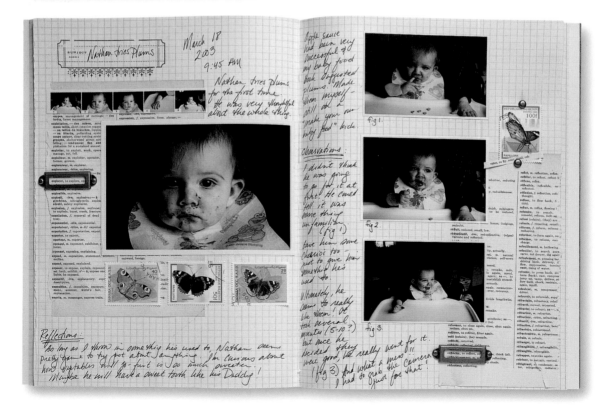

PUBLISH

A photo album does not have to be a one-of-a-kind piece. This micro-album was conceived as a printed piece that could be shared with a circle of friends and family. Commemorating the circumcision of a baby boy, an important Jewish ritual, the book serves to announce a birth, document an event, and contextualize an ancient religious practice for a new generation.

The pages were set up in a page layout program for desktop printing on 8 1/2 x 11 inch paper; the sheets are folded in half into a signature and then stapled with a long-necked stapler. (See our chapter on printed BOOKS.)
Design: Julia Reinhard Lupton
Photography:
Rosalind Reinhard

brit milah

COVENANT OF
CIRCUMCISION

Eliot Benjamin Reinhard

EMMANUEL BINJAMIN
BEN DANIEL V' RUTH

bris 30 April 2000

*The choice of a name lays claims to the present
by confronting us with a future.
Our names refer us to something beyond ourselves.*
FRANZ ROSENZWEIG

25 NISAN 5760 ENTERED INTO THE NATION OF ISRAEL THROUGH THE COVENANT OF CIRCUMCISION

ELIOT BENJAMIN REINHARD

BORN 14 MARCH
2000
4 POUNDS

C&P Telephone Yellow Pages delivers more than $50 million in sales each week in Baltimore.

18th Century muskets, bayonets, swords and pistols used in the Battle of Bennington, August 16, 1777. Selections from the outstanding military collections on exhibition at the Bennington Museum, Bennington, Vermont. Museum open all year except January and February.

Place Stamp Here:

POST CARD

Your Face Here

happy mother's day

SHENANDOAH NATIONAL PARK

Busy Persons Correspondence Card

HELLO		I SPEND MY TIME	
PAL	SUGAR	MOTORING	
FOLKS	HUBBY	HIKING	
CHUM	WIFEY	BOATING	
THIS PLACE IS		FISHING	
QUIET	NOISY	READING	
IDEAL	GRAND	LOAFING	
NOTHING EXTRA		SIGHTSEEING	
BEST ON THE MAP		BORROWING MONEY	
THE WEATHER IS		I NEED	
WARM	COOL	MONEY	YOU
WET	DRY	SLEEP	REST
PLEASANT		A GOOD JOB	
DREARY		$1,000,000	
THE FOLKS ARE		WILL SEE YOU	
NICE	SILLY	SOON	
QUIET	NOISY	LATER	
ENTERTAINING		NEXT WEEK	
FULL OF PEP		ON	
I'M FEELING		GIVE MY REGARDS TO	
FINE	WELL	MA AND DAD	
BUM	SICK	THE CHILDREN	
BLUE	HAPPY	MY CHUMS	

POST CARD

Postcards

J. Spence Holman

No longer just the stuff of vacation tell-alls, postcards have entered the correspondence vernacular in dozens of forms. You're just as likely to get one from your dentist as you are from Aunt Matilda saying how lovely Florida is this time of year. Postcards are one of the most efficient ways to get your message across, whether it's an advertisement, love letter, or invitation.

THE POINT The postcard is the lazy man's favorite correspondence—nothing to open, unfold, detach, or otherwise reconfigure just for the sake of finding out that yes, he is qualified for yet another amazing offer, and if he could just fill this out or call this number, his life would change forever. The postcard doesn't mess around. The message is right in front of your face, and within seconds, you know if it's headed for the recycling bin, the bulletin board, or your postal scrapbook. This is incredibly liberating. Just think of all the money and time we'd save if everything was a postcard. Taxes, for example, would be a breeze. We wouldn't have to suffer through exhausting Christmas card updates. Your bank statement would be easier to read. The postcard is brief, cheap, and fits in your back pocket. Mail doesn't get any better than that.

THE AUDIENCE Besides size, what differentiates the postcard from other mail is its public persona. While your mail carriers are presumably too busy to read every piece of mail that they deliver, you never know if the nosy neighbor down the hall will take a peek in your slot while you're at work. The postcard can be a vehicle for all kinds of messages, and some are well-suited for the public format. Your new product line, for example, is probably something you'd like everyone to know about, nosy or not. The latest gossip about your sister's husband's mom, however, is a different story. While you may never know exactly who sees your card, much less pays attention to it, it's important to realize that anyone could see it.

HOW TO MAIL A POSTCARD

• *The U.S. Post Office defines a postcard as 5 to 6 inches in length by 3 1/2 to 4 1/4 inches in height.*

• *A postcard must be between .007 inches and .016 inches thick.*

• *Contain the mailing address to the right 2 3/4 inches of the back of the postcard.*

• *The U.S. Post Office will affix a bar code to the bottom 5/8 inch of the back of the postcard, so leave that area clear.*

• *A return address is not required on a postcard.*

I THINK OUTSIDE THE BOX.

I AM A SUCCESS.

I LOVE MY JOB.

I AM A TEAM PLAYER.

THE BASICS

First, decide how many postcards you need. One is great for sending to a friend, but a series is great for advertising (think Burma Shave) or for retail.

Second, choose materials. Cardstock can be found at art and office supply stores, but you can use anything from mat board to corrugated cardboard to balsa wood. Make sure the card is sturdy enough to make it through the mail.

Last, apply your image and/or message. Easy reproduction methods include photocopying your image, using a rubber stamp, or printing it out on your printer.

GOOD EATS

Screen printing is a great way to mass produce your postcards. While it requires some time and skill, it is fairly inexpensive, especially if you are making dozens or hundreds. Try using a found object instead of standard cardstock. Keep your eyes open for interesting materials such as old photographs, ads, or even packaging. These recipe cards were purchased at a thrift store for less than a dollar for nearly 500.

A sticker with all of the pertinent information was designed for the back. This way, the cards can be easily reused—a new sticker can be designed and printed out for each new event.

Design: Lori Larusso and Matt Coors

THE SECRET

Just because a postcard is, well, a postcard doesn't mean that you have to give it all away for free. Accordion fold your secret message, fold a flap over it, and affix. Your message can be deeply personal, or just a nice surprise. Your correspondent will be thrilled with the sentiment, and best of all, no one will know.

Postcard design:
J. Spence Holman

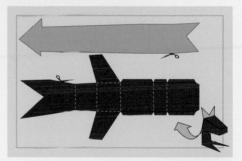

If you make it interactive, maybe they won't throw it away immediately.

Live vicariously: borrow someone else's life and impress your friends with your faux worldliness.

POWERPOINT POWER
Import Excel Charts into PowerPoint or export from Excel by choosing "save as file" or "print to a file" from the print dialog.

Now you can use a layout application to make changes. The colors, fonts, and line weights in this chart were tweaked in Adobe Illustrator.
Design: George Moore
Photography: Nancy Froehlich

DOCTOR'S
CANDY & SWEETS
EMPORIUM

101 Reasons to Eat Candy

gum disease

Presentations

George Moore

It's commonly believed that the fear of public speaking is second only to the fear of death. Chances are you'll need to face this challenge many times throughout your life, whether delivering an oral report to your classmates or pitching an idea to an investor, gallery, or community board. Today, presentations are often accompanied by digital slide shows. This chapter will show you how to design effective presentations using PowerPoint as well as a range of alternative media.

CONTENT You don't need super-flashy audiovisuals to keep your audience awake. Indeed, hyperactive graphics could distract or annoy your public rather than keeping them informed and entertained. What your presentation *does* need is a clearly organized structure, underscored and amplified with visual aids. Your support materials should not be a word-for-word transcript of what you plan to say. Instead, emphasize your main points with short, snappy text, and use visuals to add new and vital information (charts, diagrams, floor plans, photographs, video clips, and so on).

DISTRIBUTION Digital presentations do not only get shown in front of a live audience; they also get posted on the Internet, sent via e-mail, printed out and photocopied, or presented as looping media shows on kiosks in stores, exhibitions, and other public places. When you choose the medium and develop the design for your presentation, consider how it will be distributed. Do other people need to be able to open or modify your files, or is the piece entirely in your control?

COMPUTER POWER(POINT) The ubiquity of PowerPoint allows files to be shared and presented across Mac and Windows platforms. PowerPoint is handy for arranging charts of data because of its integration with spreadsheet software. This powerful tool for managing multimedia within your presentation can also be a clunky, finicky aggravation and a harbinger of bad design. Stay away from pre-made templates and whiz-bang transition effects. Start with a blank presentation and build your own clean, simple slide template.

UP'S AND DOWN'S OF POWERPOINT

• *PowerPoint provides decent integration of audio/video, but your clips need to be pre-processed for optimum performance.*

• *PowerPoint's text editor generates poorly spaced type, and if you are using special fonts, your show won't play correctly on another person's machine.*

• *Some PowerPoint users set up their text slides in PhotoShop and import them as images. This time-consuming process gives you more typographic control, but makes it harder to revise your presentation later.*

• *If your presentation will be printed out for distribution at a meeting, don't use a dark background, as it will waste toner and create pages that are tough to mark and annotate.*

• *It's easy to make hideous slide shows with little or no effort using PowerPoint's built-in templates.*

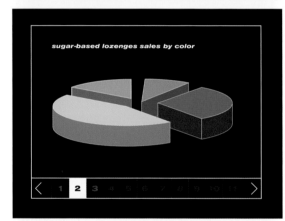

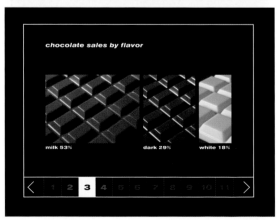

WEB-BASED PRESENTATIONS Do you know how to build a Web site? Then why not build your presentation on the Web? Flash and HTML are both flexible in scale, look, and content-handling. Your presentation can live on the Web as an archive and reference.

FLASH PRESENTATION

Produced in the animation program Flash, this presentation is a self-contained Web site. The navigation allows the user to follow a linear progression or to jump around to specific slides. The content includes charts imported from Microsoft Excel, animations explaining the distribution chain, and lots of photos of candy. Because not everyone will attend the meeting or stay awake for its entirety, the presentation will be available on the Web afterward.

DESIGNING WEB-BASED PRESENTATIONS

• *When creating a Web-based presentation, design it to live locally on the computer feeding the projector. Do not rely on an Internet connection or a CD.*

• *Projector resolutions are usually smaller than a typical computer monitor. Find out the maximum resolution beforehand or design for a screen size of 800 x 600 pixels.*

• *Keep the navigation simple and obvious, and make it as easy to run as a PowerPoint show. (Enable space-bar and arrow-key navigation as well as buttons.)*

• *Try a remote clicker, a wireless device that can control a computer or other hardware during your presentation.*

• *Avoid multiple display devices. Web-based presentations are handy for integrating a variety of media into one presentation.*

DVD PRESENTATION

A presentation stored on a DVD can be displayed on a kiosk at a store or trade fair, or distributed in a portfolio or press kit. A DVD can be played on a computer or a DVD deck. Use the DVD player's remote to wirelessly control the navigation.

Using DVD production software such as iDVD, you can include menus, videos, slideshows, and hyperlinks. Your main menu can link to clips, individual pictures, or folders of pictures. The only drawback is that standard DVD resolution (720 x 480) is slightly lower than what you can get with a computer-based presentation.

MORE ALTERNATIVES

• PDFs produced via Adobe Acrobat can be viewed as a slideshow. Produce your source file in a page layout program and export as a PDF. This process gives you total typographic control from one easy-to-modify source file. Your presentation can include hyperlinks, and your files can be easily printed, e-mailed, and posted on the Web.

• Keynote is a well-designed PowerPoint alternative for Mac users.

• Macromedia Director is an interactive animation tool that handles a wide variety of content. You can create stand-alone files that play from any computer.

• Use your digital camera. Most cameras can be plugged into a TV to display a slide show.

• Use the desktop of your laptop. If you are showing a variety of media and you don't want to create one giant presentation, set your desktop image to an appropriate graphic and use desktop aliases as buttons.

• The overhead projector is an old-school technology that still functions well. Print your computer-designed information on transparencies.

• Just use paper! You can pack a huge amount of information on a single sheet, and your audience will have something to fidget with and doodle on while you are talking.

March 2006
Media & Publicity Contact
Caroline Baker
bakerd@gmail.com
(201) 321-8907

Going Public: A Do-It-Yourself Guide to
Graphic Design by Ellen Lupton
Release Date: September 2005
Book Party: September 20th, 2005 from 6-10 pm

Have you ever asked a friend you consider to be more creative than yourself to do you a favor,
like designing a business card for your step-mom who's starting a fruit-basket company?
More than likely you got the response "Do it yourself." Did you stop dead your tracks unsure
how to proceed? Now you can give your atrophied creative muscles the workout they deserve,
with the new guide to design, Going Public: A Do-It-Yourself Guide to Design.

Press kits

Alissa Faden and Veronica Semeco

You're a collector of tiki *tzotchkes* who just scored a showing at a Maui community center. You're a retired Girl Scout opening a cookie shop. You're looking to move your band out of the garage and onto the stage. You're someone—anyone—who needs to get the word out and snag attention from the media. You're someone who needs to make a *press kit*, a marketing tool designed to draw media attention to your endeavors. A press kit provides journalists with the who, what, when, where, and why of your project, making it easy for them to contact you and publish vivid and accurate information about what you are doing.

THE FOLDER With a little ingenuity, an impressive press kit package is possible on any budget. Keep in mind how many you'll be sending out, so that you don't plan for something unrealistic. Unless you have an army of cousins at your disposal, your time and budget will be constraining factors. The folder at left requires handwork, while the folders on the following pages use store bought supplies or commercial print services.

THE PRESS RELEASE The *press release* is a concise document illuminating what makes your story news, printed on a letterhead featuring your logo and contact information. The most important facts should appear in the first paragraph; this text might be used directly by journalist to create event listings for a local paper. Include dates and location if an event is involved. Your release should take a tone suitable for your event and include first-person quotes for journalists to use in articles.

PARTY BAG FOLDER
This fun folder is made from a gift bag that you can buy at a party supply or paper store. The front flips open to reveal pockets to hold press materials inside.
Design: Veronica Semeco
Photography: Nancy Froehlich

PLANNING A SUCCESSFUL PRESS KIT

- *Send kits early; reporters need planning time. Send four months ahead for monthly magazines; one month ahead for weekly or daily publications.*

- *One reliable person should be listed as the primary contact. If your contact info is hard to find, you won't be found either.*

- *Create an on-line companion to your kit.*

Journalists can go to your Web site to cut-and-paste text, download pictures, or listen to music.

- *Maintaining a core set of colors gives the kit a cohesive feel.*

- *Make follow up calls. Assume that the journalist is overloaded. Collect your thoughts before you dial. Keep the call short.*

CONTENT CHECKLIST

- *folder*
- *package for mailing (express recommended)*
- *well-written release*
- *photos/reel/audio CD*
- *press clippings*
- *biography/resume*
- *promotional souvenir (magnet, pin, bumper sticker, balloon)*

READYMADE PRESS KIT
This press kit has been produced using low-cost, off-the-shelf office supplies. Everything can be photocopied or desktop printed. Play around with colored paper and bright folders. Find innovative uses for generic materials. Simple objects such as pens, pins, erasers, balloons, or bumper stickers can make your kit memorable and physically appealing.
Design: Veronica Semeco
Photography: Dan Meyers

February 2006
Media & Publicity Contact
Veronica Semeco
Veronica@BodyBlock.com
(410) 829-4839

Live Healthy Organization in conjuction with
the Eating Disorder Reasearch Center and Springfield College present:

The Third Annual Every Body's Block Party Day

A Street Fair Focusing on Health and Body Acceptance
Friday, May 23–Sunday, May 25. Open 11:30 am–11pm

From May 23 to May 25, students, faculty, staff, and the Springfield community will gather and motivate
each other to take action and make promoting healthy body image part of their everyday lives. At Every Body's
Block Party, the Live Healthy Organization will promote healthy body images for Springfield's citizens. This
year's celebration will feature national spokespeople for the campaign and the re-launch of the campaign Web site.

Since its creation in 2001, the Every Body's Campaign has spoken out against offensive advertisements
media images that harm the public perception of the human body. While promoting positive advertising
business world, the group also organizes free discussion groups where citizens can talk about their bodies.

every BodY's BLOCK PaRtY

Presented by Live Healthy Organization
in conjuction with Eating Disorder
Reasearch Center and Springfield College

A Street Fair Focusing on
Health and Body Acceptance
Friday, May 23–Sunday, May 25
Open 11:30 am–11pm

POSTER AS PRESS FOLDER
This press kit design uses a band's commercially printed tour poster as a folder. This design presumes a reasonable budget for commercial printing, but it makes double use of resources.
Design: Alissa Faden
Photography: Dan Meyers

①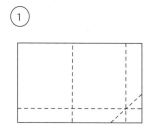

②

③

④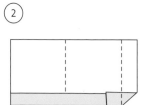

KIWI ⊛ TRUST

Musical Mayh[...]
1971 Santa M[...]
Los Angeles, [...]

**Press Conta[...]
Audra Kidma[...]**
(917) 684-837[...]
Press@Music[...]

Interview Re[...]
OnAir@Music[...]

August 2005

**MUSICAL MAYHEM GROUP INTRODUCES
KIWI TRUST
American Tour October 2005–January 2006**
Including Special New Year's Mayhem Extravaganza Dec. 31

Who are they? They are New Zealanders; Kiwis if you like.

The Kiwi Trust is an unprecedented success story on its native continent. For this group of tan surfers with irresistible accents, music always came naturally. Jonathan, Reggie and Mark have been playing wedding gigs since the age of 14. It didn't take long before they went from the chapel to the top of the Auckland and Sydney charts. Frontman Jonathan Fresham explains the band's desire to now go [wor]ld wide and reach a broader audience: "It is not enough just to be [...] the Outback. People in the United States know the Outback [... f]oremost as a steakhouse. We want to change that. Or at [... the] Bloomin' Onion a run for its money." The Kiwis take [... r]oots and will concentrate on maintaining their cultural [... w]orking their way into the American indie scene.

[...]signed to the small power-house label Music [... m]ake the transition. Other Music Mayhem imports [...]Quad Beat and The Cravats. For Kiwi Trust, [...]October starting with small venues and then [... sw]eep through larger venues once buzz spreads. [...]musician who complains about touring is a "total [...]have the opportunity to chat one on one with his [... mu]ltiple times when a fan's anecdote has inspired a

[...]'s sound is difficult to pin down because they are such a [... gro]up. They're an educated bunch that focuses on lyrics. [...]have a striking semblance to the Beatles, but then they'll [... so]ng that sounds so hard rock, it'll throw you off. A[...] [... rea]dy to feel a strong desire to stay hot on the [...]

Reggie – Guitar

My chums roped me
[...]

Mark – Vocals

I can sing, I can [...]
and I see each [...]

KIWI TRUST
Musical Mayhem Artist Group
1971 Santa Monica Blvd. #300
Los Angeles, CA 90048 U.S.A.

Audra Kidman, Press Man[...]
office: (917) 684-6375
cellular: (917) 867-5903
Audra@MusicalMayhe[...]

December 24, 31 ...... New Y[...]
January 13 ...... Balti[...]

Stationery

Veronica Semeco

From the cover letters you send out to get a job, to the invoices you mail to get paid, your communications should be printed on stationery that reflects your personal or professional identity. You can have letterhead and envelopes commercially printed on matching paper and envelopes, or you can produce your stationery on the fly using your desktop printer or other ready-to-hand materials and processes. Designing your own stationery is an opportunity to express your personal brand through imagery, typefaces, and materials. Set yourself loose in a deluxe paper store or an ordinary office warehouse, and build your own self-portrait in paper.

THE LETTERHEAD is the core of your stationery program. A letterhead typically includes the name, address, phone number, and e-mail contact for an individual, business, or organization. Include your logo if you have one. Letters printed on letterhead are considered official documents; a reference from a school or a warning from a lawyer uses letterhead to establish the legitimacy of the content. Likewise, when you send out bills to your clients or inquiries to potential employers, a well-designed letterhead reflects your seriousness of purpose.

PERSONAL NOTEPAPER can be more informal than a letterhead, presenting only your name or a simple image. Attach a handwritten message to a report, paper, book, CD, or other document, or use it to send personal letters or thank-you notes. We recommend printing notepaper on a smaller size than standard letter paper, such as 5 1/2 by 8 1/2 inches (half sheet).

BUSINESS CARDS can be coordinated with your letterhead; see our BUSINESS CARD chapter.

ENVELOPES come in many sizes, and they can be annoying to run through a desktop printer. Plan your design in one or two useful sizes to avoid endless formatting headaches. The standard business size is Number 10 (9 1/2 x 4 1/8 inches). We also like booklet size (6 1/2 x 9 1/2 inches), which holds a standard letter-sized sheet folded in half. When designing envelopes, consider what you will be mailing. You may need a larger envelope for sending out press kits or proposals. For more information on designing envelopes, see our ENVELOPE chapter.

LABELS are a handy alternative to printed envelopes, as they can be applied to packages, folders, and envelopes of any size. Labels make it easy to reuse old boxes and packing envelopes. Depending on your needs, you may want to produce CD labels as part of your overall stationery package. (Don't send out your digital portfolio on a disk marked in Sharpie.) Labels in numerous sizes are available at office supply stores; you can also make your own using adhesives or clear packing tape.

Veronica Semeco
Flowers - Home Décor
1604 Park Ave. #4
Hollywood, FL 23456

Veronica Semeco

Flowers - Home Décor
1604 Park Ave. #4
Hollywood, FL 23456
phone: 410.669.7512
email: vsemeco@wahoo.com

USE A WORD PROCESSOR
Letterheads and envelopes
can be designed and
printed from the computer
workstation in your home
or office. You can set up a
letterhead as a template in
a word processing program
such as Microsoft Word, or in
a sophisticated page layout
program such as Adobe
InDesign. Use interesting
paper and techniques such
as hole-punching to give
your letterhead a distinctive
physical character.
Design: Veronica Semeco

Veronica Semeco
1604 Park Ave. #4
Hollywood, FL 23456

Veronica Semeco
1604 Park Ave. #4
Hollywood, FL 23456

Veronica Semeco | Interior Designer
1604 Park Ave. #4 Hollywood, Fl 23456 phone: 410.669.7512 email: vsemeco@wahoo.com

Veronica Semeco | Interior Designer
1604 Park Ave. #4 Hollywood, Fl 23456 phone: 410.669.7512 email: vsemeco@wahoo.com

Veronica Semeco · PHOTOGRAPHY
1604 Park ave. #4
Hollywood, FL 23456

Veronica Semeco · Vetinarian
1604 Park Ave. #4
Hollywood, FL 23456

Veronica Semeco · DJ
1604 Park Ave. #4
Hollywood, FL 23456

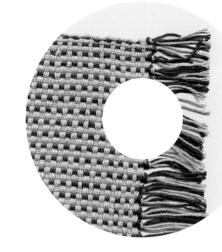

USE LABELS

Make any envelope match your own personal identity with adhesive labels. Create simple shapes with the drawing tools in your software program, or look through your closets and shoe boxes to find photographs, maps, magazine pages, or drawings with interesting textures and patterns. You can put fabrics and small objects directly on your scanner to create instant high-resolution photography. Insert images into a word-processing or page layout file, and combine them with typography. Save the file as a template and use it any time.
Design: Veronica Semeco

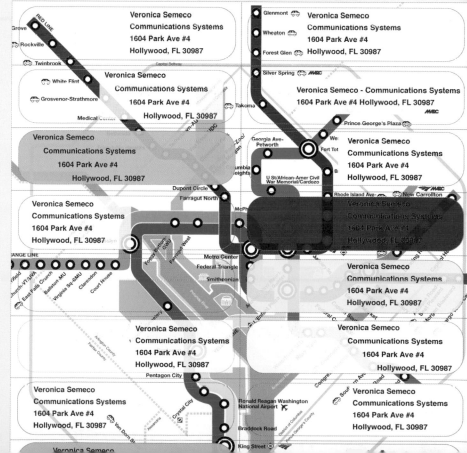

PAPER, SCISSORS & GLUE
Glue strips of patterned
paper to paper, envelopes,
and cards to make personal
stationery.
Design: Veronica Semeco
Photography: Dan Meyers

SURFACES

Put your mark on different surfaces by screen printing or rubber-stamping. The image stays the same, while the material keeps changing.
Design: Veronica Semeco
Photography: Dan Meyers

Stickers

Adam Palmer

Inspired by street art such as graffiti and posters, stickers have become a fast-moving artistic medium. Free downloadable files are posted on the Internet and are available to print and stick anywhere, anytime. A sticker designed in Baltimore today could end up on a road sign in Tokyo tomorrow. Along the way, the interpretation of a sticker shifts as it moves through different cultures. Use this global urban phenomenon to push a cause, promote an event, or simply share your art. Stickers also make great give-aways, party favors, invitations, and more.

PRINT AND STICK The easiest way to make a sticker is with a desktop printer and an 8.5 x 11 sheet of blank sticker paper (label stock), which can be purchased at an office supply store. Print your graphic, cut around the edge, peel off the backing, and then place your sticker wherever you want it to be seen!

Sticker-making kits use pressure to apply a laminate and an adhesive backing to any flat, flexible surface. This option allows you to print your sticker on any paper you want. Sticker makers (such as Xryon) are available online and at craft stores. If you need a large volume of stickers, have them printed and cut commercially.

MEAT & VEGGIES
Joe likes his meat, and he wants everyone to know it. Using his sticker know-how, he plastered his flashy hunk of cowhide all over town. Boy, did that stir up Sally and her veggie-loving friends. Before you knew it, there was an all-out urban sticker war between the two sides. People in the streets and on the subways everywhere started to take notice.
Design: Adam Palmer
Photography: Nancy Froehlich

WATERPROOFING

Stickers printed via ink jet will bleed if left unprotected in the rain and snow. However, printing on glossy paper will make the stickers last longer.

Choose outdoor placement carefully, such as under an awning or on the inside window of a newspaper box. Commercially printed stickers use waterproof inks.

The ultimate protection for stickers is lamination, which will also make your stickers more expensive.

POST & DOWNLOAD

Make your stickers available to the masses. Save or scan your artwork as a PDF file and post on a Web site. Anyone can download and print your art. Include crop marks for square-shaped stickers to make cutting easier. If your stickers have an organic shape, use a thick, black border to make trimming easier. The border will also help your sticker stand out.

and peel

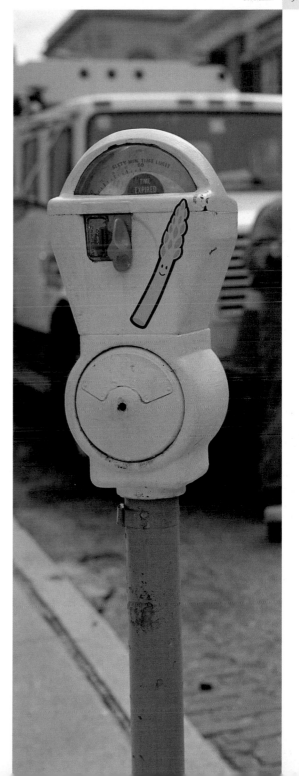

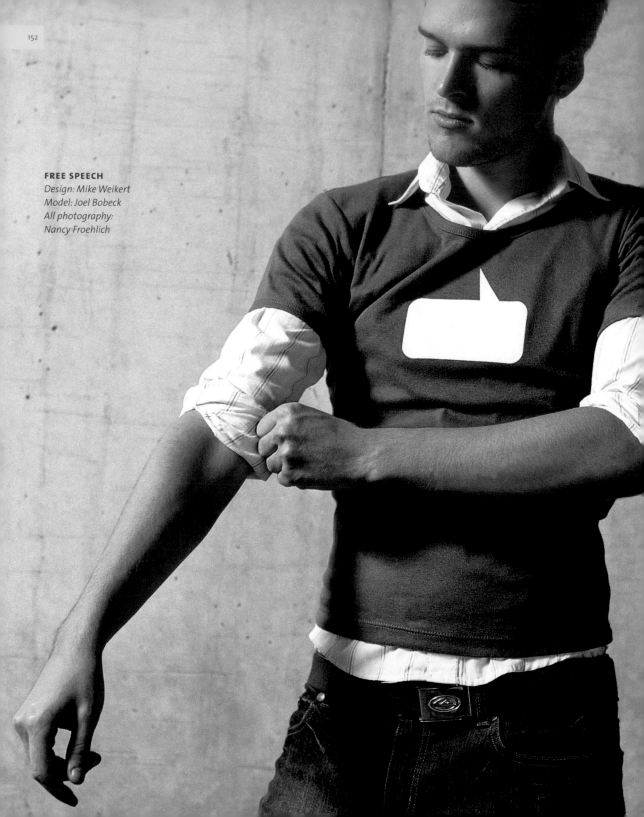

FREE SPEECH
Design: Mike Weikert
Model: Joel Bobeck
All photography:
Nancy Froehlich

T-Shirts

Ellen Lupton

The basic cotton undershirt went public in 1955, when James Dean wore a plain white t-shirt in *Rebel without a Cause*. Shirts printed with pictures and slogans became essential street wear in the 1960s, and some of today's most creative graphic designers view the t-shirt as a vital form of art and communication. Fashion designers continually experiment with the shape, drape, and proportions of this utilitarian classic. You can use a variety of techniques—geared for short-run and long-run production—to try your own hand at t-shirt design.

SILKSCREEN Most commercially-printed shirts are produced with a silkscreen, a device consisting of a fine-meshed fabric stretched tautly around a frame. Parts of the screen are blocked off, and ink is pressed through the open areas. Each color requires its own screen. You will pay a one-time set-up charge for each screen in addition to the cost of printing each shirt. The set-up charge is spread out across the print run, becoming less significant the more shirts you print.

There are companies in every metropolitan area that provide printed shirts (as well as bags, hats, and other items) to schools, businesses, clubs, and individuals. The printer will provide you with the shirts at a wholesale price as well as printing them for you. You can also learn to screenprint with your own equipment.

DESIGNING FOR THE SILKSCREEN PROCESS

• *Unlike iron-on transfer paper, a silkscreened design will print cleanly, without any background texture.*

• *Whereas transfer film is transparent, silkscreen ink is opaque, making it possible to print light inks on dark fabrics. (You will pay a little more for this, however, because an extra hit of white is needed to make the color completely opaque.)*

• *Avoid tiny type and finely detailed, high-resolution images and designs.*

• *Communicate with your printer throughout the job so there are no surprises at the end. Printing over seams or onto pockets, for example, can raise the cost of your project.*

• *Silkscreen printers usually want a vector file, with type converted to outlines. Adobe Illustrator and Macromedia Freehand are typical software applications for making such files.*

• *Always provide your printer with a paper proof of your graphic at the exact size that it will be reproduced. Tape a printout of the graphic to a sample shirt to indicate positioning. (Your printer may assume that you want a monster-sized graphic across the middle of the shirt, when what you really want is a discreet image just above the bustline.)*

• *For an extra cost, you can order a printed sample before proceeding with the whole job. This cost is worthwhile for a big project. You would hate to foot the bill for dozens of misprinted t-shirts.*

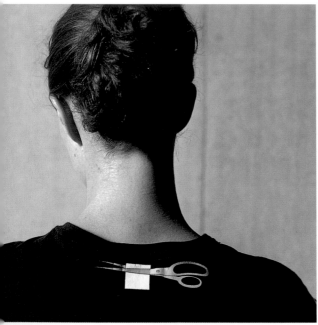

IRON-ON TRANSFERS are an economical way to apply your own graphics or photographic images to a t-shirt. Just create a graphic with the software of your choice and print onto transfer paper with an ink-jet printer. Apply to shirt following the manufacturer's instructions.

DESIGNING FOR THE TRANSFER PROCESS

• *Transfer paper is available for dark or light colored fabric. Light fabric transfers are transparent, so the color of the shirt will always show through. Dark fabric transfers are opaque.*

• *When using light fabric transfers, flip your design horizontally to print. With dark fabric transfers, don't flip the art.*

• *If applying your graphic close to the seam or on a tricky location like the arm (see designs to left) put a piece of cardboard inside the shirt before ironing. This will keep seams on the other side from getting in the way.*

• *The transfer material has its own texture, which you need to account for in your design. Putting a border around a block of text or a line drawing, for example, draws attention away from the background surface of the transfer film.*

• *Test your design on an actual shirt before printing it out in quantity.*

• *Transfer designs are less durable than silkscreened ones. If you are selling your shirts or giving them as gifts, include washing instructions (found in manufacturer's directions).*

• *Ironing requires time and patience, so a large-volume project should be silkscreened. Alternatively, a commercial shirt company can produce the transfers and apply them with an industrial heat press.*

• *Share your transfer designs with other people by posting PDFs on the Web.*

NO-TAG
Designer and model:
Michelle Brooks

MOM TATTOO
Designers and models:
Mike and Maya Weikert

IRON-ON TRANSFERS

DO-IT-YOURSELF
Design: Zvezdena Rogic
Model: Viviane von der Heydt

FOLLOW THESE
INSTRUCTIONS TO A TEE
Designer and Model:
Alissa Faden

MAKE ART NOT WAR
Design: Allen Harrison
Models: Andrew Newman and
Sonam Sapra

BUSHOCCHIO
Design: Kristen Spilman
Model: Seth Rosati

BLEACHED TEXT

Materials: household bleach, cotton swabs and/or natural-haired paintbrush

1. Plan your design on paper and test on a scrap shirt.

2. Put cardboard inside shirt to protect opposite side. Work in a well-ventilated area.

3. Paint your design onto the shirt with undiluted bleach, using either cotton swabs or a natural-haired paintbrush. (A synthetic brush disintegrates in the bleach.) Wear gloves.

3. It may take a few minutes to see results. As the bleach dries, the effect will become more dramatic.

4. Flush bleach down drain with plenty of water. Allow the shirt to completely dry before handling. Wash separately before wearing.

Designer and model:
Kimberly Bost
Photography: Nancy Froehlich

YOU ARE WHERE YOU WORK

Materials: rubber stamp, ink pad

1. Go to work.

2. Find a rubber stamp ("Draft," "Return to Sender," "Original," "Paid," "Void," etc.). Date and mail-routing stamps may also be available.

2. Stamp your shirt at work, or borrow stamps for later.

3. Put stamp(s) back where you found them.

4. The ink will disappear after a few washings. Print a new shirt every week or two.

Design: Spence Holman

OTHER TECHNIQUES In addition to these standard printing methods, there are other ways to apply imagery to a t-shirt.

- *See* MACHINE EMBROIDERY *chapter for guidelines concerning this intriguing industrial process.*

- *Fabric markers, Sharpies, and ballpoint pen are better for tote bags than t-shirts, as they don't withstand repeated washing.*

- *Sew an image onto a shirt, bag, or other object to give the surface a physical character. The image itself could be silkscreened, transfer printed, or "found" on existing fabric.*

EMERGENCY VELCRO

Materials: emergency item, Velcro, needle and thread

1. Choose an emergency item for your shirt (aspirin, pencil, post-it, etc), or assemble a collection of items and exchange them as needed.

2. Cut a piece of Velcro, about 1/2 x 1/2 inches.

3. Stitch the soft side of the Velcro to the shirt.

4. Sew or glue other side of the Velcro to the emergency item.

Designer and model:
Veronica Semeco

DE-BRANDED

Materials: tracing paper, contact paper, acrylic matte medium (used for thinning acrylic artist's paint), paint brush, screen printing ink, printed t-shirt

1. Trace image on t-shirt with tracing paper. Cut out and transfer to contact paper.

2. Cut shape out of the contact paper, leaving a 3 inch border.

3. Adhere contact paper, so image area becomes the only space available for painting. Apply 3-4 layers of matte medium around edge of image area, painting from the outside in (this seals contact paper to shirt). Allow each layer to dry completely.

4. Paint screenprinting ink to image area until covered.

5. Let dry completely before removing stencil.

Design: Chris Jackson
Model: Adam Savermilch

BITMAP ALIEN

Materials: spray paint, graph paper, Xacto knife, double-sided tape, dye (optional)

1. Design your own alien by marking off a 6-inch square on graph paper. Fill squares to create alien. Leave 1 inch around edge.

2. Cut out alien with an Xacto knife. Then cut out the square window around alien.

3. Dye shirt (optional). Dye is available in the detergent aisle at the supermarket.

4. Lay shirt flat in a spray paint-safe area. Using double-sided tape, attach alien and square onto shirt.

5. Spray paint and let dry.

Design: Adam Palmer
Model: Elina Asanti

MAKE IT FIT

Materials: thread, sewing machine, safety pins

1. On an oversized sweatshirt, gather and pin one inch of fabric along the front from the neck down to the waist.

2. Sew along line. Repeat steps 1 and 2 on the back of shirt.

3. Try on the shirt, and continue to sew in one-inch (or so) increments until it fits, keeping an equal number of seams on the front and back.

4. Cut the neckline and sleeves. (Use your favorite t-shirt as a template.)

ALTERING THE SHIRT ITSELF A t-shirt is a generic industrial product that can be altered to fit your body and personal style. It is the fashion equivalent of 8.5 x 11 paper. You can approach these projects with subtle tailoring (no one will know the shirt wasn't manufactured that way), or you can let it be obvious that you did it yourself.

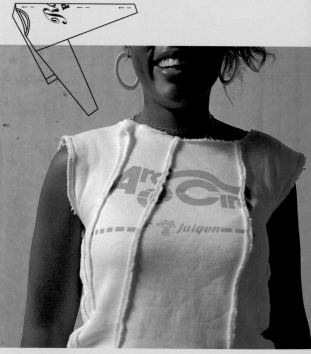

DESIGNING A CUSTOM-CUT SHIRT

• *Women like to cut the thick, ribbed collars out of standard t-shirts to make a sexier neckline. Neatly follow the edge of the existing collar, or devise your own shape. (Practice first on a worn-out shirt.)*

• *To make a men's sleeveless ribbed undershirt fit a woman's body better, fold over the fabric on the shoulders, creating smaller arm holes.*

• *Use simple cuts to adjust the shape of the sleeves and the overall length of the shirt. Hem the edges, or leave them raw.*

• *You can choose to make stitches discreet, decorative, or brutally obvious.*

• *Try asymmetrical as well as symmetrical designs.*

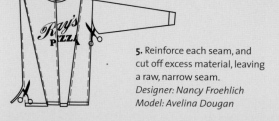

5. Reinforce each seam, and cut off excess material, leaving a raw, narrow seam.
Designer: Nancy Froehlich
Model: Avelina Dougan

KNITTED SHOULDER WRAP
Materials: yarn, knitting needles (or old scarf), elastic, safety pins, needle, thread
1. Choose spot on chest for the top of the knitted shoulder wrap, about 2-3 inches below collarbone. From there, measure around your body. This length is *n*.
2. Knit a shoulder wrap that is 6 inches wide and *n* inches long. Attach ends.

3. Cut a 1-inch-wide elastic band at *n*. Sew ends together. Sew a piece of scrap fabric around elastic.
4. Cut off the top portion of a sleeveless t-shirt at spot of first *n* measurement.
5. Sew the top of shoulder wrap to elastic banding. Attach piece to t-shirt with safety pins. Detach the shoulder wrap when washing.
(Don't know how to knit? Alter an old scarf.)
Designer and model: Katherine Cornelius

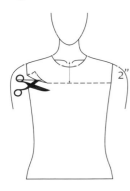

FLOWER ACCESSORY
Materials: needle, thread
1. Draw a 10 x 20 rectangle on an old T-shirt and cut it out.
2. Cut a wavy pattern around the edge of the rectangle and an oval from the middle.
3. Gather fabric as you weave needle through the bottom of the petal shapes. Halfway through the pattern, tie off to form the inner petals.
4. Bring the remaining fabric up and around the inner petals. Gather and shift the fabric into place until the desired look is achieved.
5. Stitch back and forth across the bottom area of your flower to secure the outer petals and the total flower. Tie off.
6. Use a safety pin to secure it to a garment or bag.
Designer and model: Ida Woldemichael

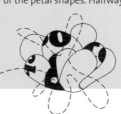

Tote bags

Katherine Cornelius

People of all ages use bags to carry and hold materials, but totes are more than just functional. They're fun, expressive, and easy to personalize. Keep several totes in your closet, one for each mood and activity. Before you spend all your cash on a new designer tote, think outside the bag and make your own. In addition to such methods as screen printing, embroidery, and iron-on transfers, try the one-of-a-kind ideas shown here.

SCREAM

Take a photo or find an existing image to use on the bag. Use image-editing software such as Adobe PhotoShop to change the digital image to Grayscale. Adjust Brightness/Contrast so that there are two strong areas, one black and one white. Print to size and cut out area that will be painted. Attach stencil to bag tightly and spraypaint.
Design: Zvezdana Rogic

POWER BAG

Ever wonder what to do with your colorful printed calendar when the year comes to a close? Make a cool clear tote. Buy clear vinyl at a fabric store, and sew pieces together in intervals to create pockets. Cut up old calendars or other graphic materials and slip them into the openings. If you want, add useful things like shopping lists and metro cards.
Design: Katherine Cornelius
Photography: Nancy Froehlich

ALPHABET SOUP

Buy rubber stamps at a craft store and have fun making a pattern or message. Canvas is a great material to work with, although any surface will do. Shown here are a printed tote and matching belt.
Design: Katherine Cornelius
Photography: Nancy Froehlich

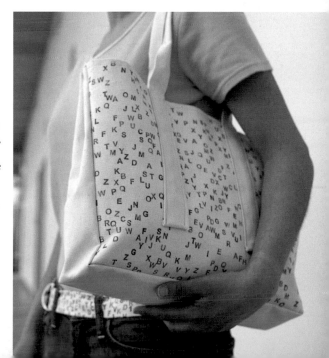

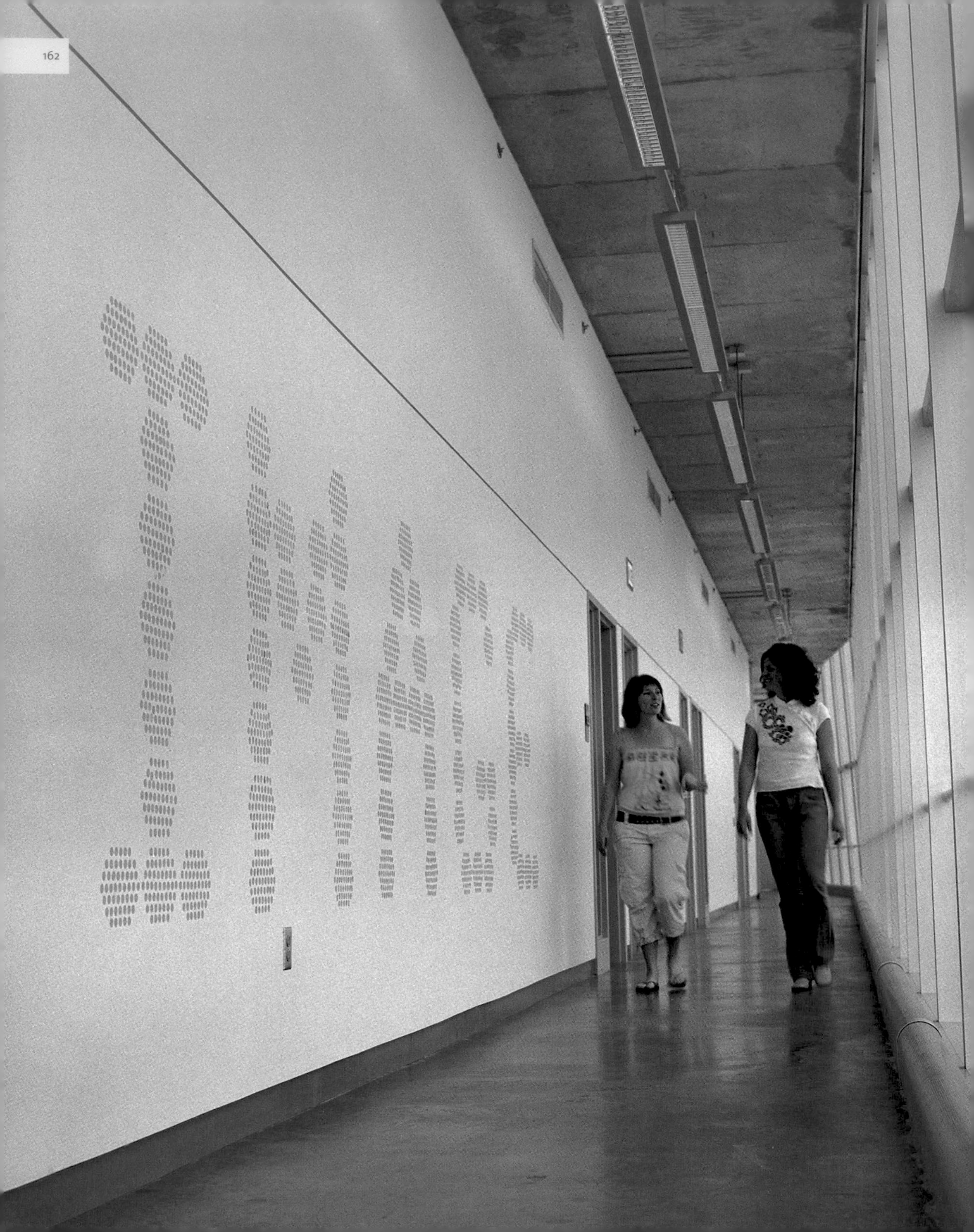

Wall graphics

Kimberly Bost

Wall graphics can provide information and establish an atmosphere in retail spaces, office areas, cafes, and exhibitions as well as in dorm rooms and apartments. You can make your own wall graphics with everyday materials such as contact paper and office labels, or you can work with a commercial sign company to create adhesive vinyl graphics from a digital illustration file. Whether used as decoration or to convey a specific message, large-scale graphics transform a flat wall into a billboard or a work of art.

OFFICE LABELS For an inexpensive approach to producing wall graphics, use office labels to create imagery or text. (Note that office labels are difficult to remove from glass, but are usually easy to remove from latex-painted walls. Test your surface to be sure.)

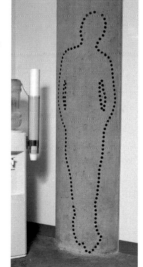

WORD IMAGE
The word "image" was constructed using ¾-inch circular office labels. Each letter is made from a series of large dots. Each large dot is composed of a group of small office label dots.

Create a pattern to construct each circle in the letter, then measure and tape the boundaries of the letters on the wall. Eye or mark the placement of each dot using the pattern as a guide or a stencil.

When designing your graphic, keep in mind the size of the label you will be using, so that you can determine how many labels you will need. It can be helpful to map your graphic onto a grid of dots and then subtract the negative space from the grid to form the image.

Apply labels to clean surface. For a complex design, use an overhead projector, you can project a transparent mock-up of your design on the wall. Alternately, translate the design from paper to the wall by making a grid in pencil or tape.
Design: Kim Bost

WATER COOLER GUY
Outline a figure in office label dots. Now, there is always someone to talk to around the water cooler.
Design: Judy Cheng

Photography: Nancy Froehlich

PLANNING WALL GRAPHICS

• Measure the space the graphic will live in. Create your design to scale; for example, one inch equals one foot.

• Mock up your design on a digital photograph. This is an easy way to get a sense of how your graphic will look in the space, and it will help you explain your design to other people who may need to see it.

• Be sure to mock up your design at actual size, and look at it in the space. Just tape a printout to the wall. Inexperienced designers often make wall text bigger than it needs to be.

• Use paint to enhance the effect of applied graphics or to transform the character of an entire space. Paint walls different colors or create stripes or zones of different colors.

• When placing graphics, consider the eye level of the viewer. Museums and galleries hang paintings so that the center is 59 or 60 inches from the floor. Depending on the function of your graphics, you may want to place them higher than eye level (to create a "title" for an overall space) or lower (if the room's occupants will primarily be seated).

CONTACT PAPER Self-adhesive paper is an easy-to-use, inexpensive material that is available in many colors and patterns. Contact paper can wrap around corners, and it can be applied to floors (temporarily) or windows, as well as to painted walls. Teacher-supply companies may have more colors available than your local hardware store.

THINK RELAX
The words "think" and "relax" were cut from contact paper to provide atmosphere in a student lounge. You can work from an exact plan (lettering, logos, geometric elements), or you can cut free-form patterns on the fly (leaves, flowers, birds, clouds, blobs). When creating text, avoid small or complex letterforms and large quantities of text. Place a printed version of your design on top of the contact paper to use as a cutting guide. Secure the printout with tape. Cut through the printout and the contact paper using an Xacto knife or scissors and apply graphics to a clean surface. *Design: Kim Bost*

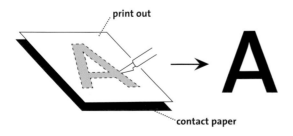

print out

contact paper

CUT VINYL Many commercial signs are created with cut vinyl, a self-adhesive material that is cut to follow the vectors of a graphics file. Signage companies can work directly from your files. They can also provide printed vinyl, cling-on graphics, and banners for indoor or outdoor use.

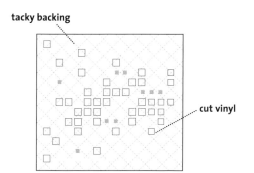

tacky backing

cut vinyl

VINYL PIXELS

This wall graphic was produced by a signage company with custom cut vinyl. Create your design with a vector-based program such as Adobe Illustrator or Corel Draw and provide the file in the format specified by the sign company. Typically, you will be asked to convert all lettering to outlines, so that the company doesn't need access to your fonts. Position graphic on the wall using the low-tack backing sheet that is provided with the cut vinyl. Burnish the graphics into place and remove backing.
Design: Kimberly Bost

Web sites

Katherine Cornelius and Allen Harrison

For relatively little money, anyone with access to a networked computer can produce a Web site, zine, or blog and connect with people all over the world. This chapter will introduce you to publishing your own content in a simple Web site, from pre-planning to design to the basics of HTML and other technologies.

Make a Plan

Before you turn your computer on, sit down with a pencil and paper and plan your Web site. This will save you time and energy in the long run and will lead to a more enjoyable experience.

GOALS AND AUDIENCES List the top three to five goals of your Web project, in order of importance. Your main goal may be to sell your artwork, share your opinions, build a photo gallery, or promote an event.

Next, describe the intended audiences. Are they young or old? What Web sites do they visit? What is their typical connection speed to the Internet? How much time will they spend on your Web site?

These exercises will keep you focused throughout the Web development process. When you are deciding to add a new feature to the site, refer back to your goals to check the relevance. Use your audiences to make decisions such as the placement of content, font size, and use of bandwidth-heavy technology.

SITE ARCHITECTURE Diagram the hierarchy of your content. You can do this on the computer, as we did in our example, or with pencil and paper. Connect the main topics to the home page, then connect the subsections to the main topics. These connections will be links, or pathways for users to reach the content.

When completed, think as if you were an end-user. How quickly can you find certain content? What information needs to be linked to the home page? Keep in mind how your audience will use the information. What will they be looking for? What will interest them?

FILE STRUCTURE When designing your site, always remember that a Web site is a collection of files. Every page on the site is a file, and so is every graphic or movie. Each file has its own name and location (address). The browser reads all those names and addresses and builds a page on your screen. Your site architecture is a blueprint of the way the files will sit on your hard drive and on the server. Use this blueprint when you are creating HTML files.

To explain the Web process, we created several examples of home pages for an imaginary Web site. Listed below are our goals and audience for our fictional site.

OUR GOALS	OUR AUDIENCES
1. Create a visual tutorial and useful tool about Web design.	*1. Technically savvy people who may not be trained as designers.*
2. Create designs that are fun and engaging.	*2. People with a general interest in design.*
3. Present examples that do not require a lot of technical knowledge.	*3. People who want to grasp the power to publish in their own hands.*

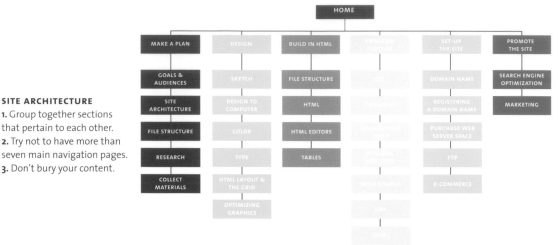

SITE ARCHITECTURE
1. Group together sections that pertain to each other.
2. Try not to have more than seven main navigation pages.
3. Don't bury your content.

RESEARCH Find Web sites that you like and ask yourself why they are successful. Look at the design and placement of navigation elements and the use of colors and typefaces. Look for Web sites that are similar in audience, subject matter, or look and feel to your future Web site. Look for simple sites that are not too far beyond your technical ability.

COLLECT MATERIALS AND CONTENT Transfer photos and art work to digital format. Save graphics as JPEGs and GIFs. Gather these materials before you start the design process so that you can use them in your design or as inspiration.

You also need to assemble your written content early in the Web process. Delays are often caused by missing content. Save the copy in text documents; you can copy and paste into HTML later in the process.

Design

SKETCH On paper, sketch several layouts for your home page and interior pages. Try different placements of the logo (or header), navigation, and content. Plan how the navigation will change on the interior pages.

TAKING YOUR DESIGN TO THE COMPUTER The standard image-editing software for building a Web site is Adobe PhotoShop. Use it to make shapes, choose colors, crop images, type content, and save files for the Web.

Start by creating a document that is 750 pixels wide x 480 pixels high. This size will fit into the standard Web resolution of 800 x 600 pixels and will allow users to print the pages of your site. Next, place the design elements in the locations indicated in your sketch.

COLOR Choose a color scheme that matches the feel of your site. It could be serious or fun, warm or cool. Use contrasting colors to highlight certain features. It is important that your image files are saved in RGB, since this is the format computer monitors use to read colors.

TYPE There are two main ways to display text on the Web: HTML text and graphic text. HTML text is written in an HTML document. There are only a handful of fonts that are displayed on all platforms. Common HTML typefaces are Times, Arial, Helvetica, Verdana, Courier, and Georgia. Graphic text is created in an image-editing software tool such as PhotoShop and is displayed as an image.

Use HTML text for large bodies of copy and text that you want to download quickly. Use graphic text when you want to use a specific font or integrate type with an image. Navigation and header images are commonly in graphic text. Text is best saved as a gif file.

HTML LAYOUT AND THE GRID The designs that you have created on the computer will be broken down into components of an HTML page. As you work, think about how the design will translate into HTML. Most HTML layouts use tables with rows and columns. If this is your first Web site, you may want to design using a simple grid.

OPTIMIZING GRAPHICS FOR THE WEB Web professionals use programs such as Adobe ImageReady (companion to Adobe PhotoShop) and Macromedia Fireworks to optimize and save images. These programs allow you to optimize multiple images at a time and save them to your images folder. This is especially helpful for rollover navigation images.

TOOLS OF THE TRADE
The plywood, hands, pencil, and ruler are part of a background image created with a digital camera. The title and navigation were produced in PhotoShop and saved as optimized gifs. The body copy is HTML text.
Design: Katherine Cornelius

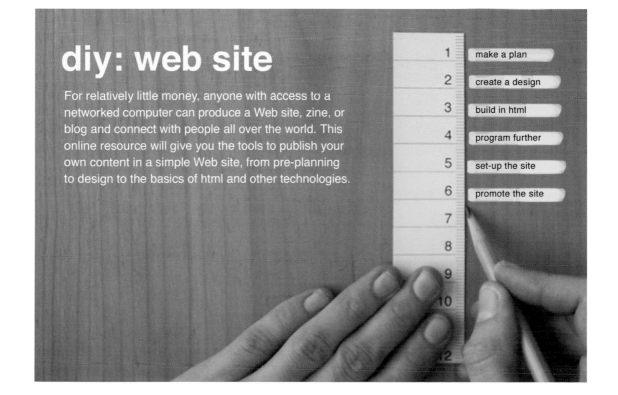

diy: web site

For relatively little money, anyone with access to a networked computer can produce a Web site, zine, or blog and connect with people all over the world. This online resource will give you the tools to publish your own content in a simple Web site, from pre-planning to design to the basics of html and other technologies.

1 make a plan
2 create a design
3 build in html
4 program further
5 set-up the site
6 promote the site

Build in HTML

FILE STRUCTURE When building a Web site, it is important to organize your files and graphics in a simple, consistent way. On your local computer, create a new folder with the name of your project. Do not use any spaces or special characters in the folder or file names; use the underscore character to separate words. We suggest creating three folders inside the main folder; name the folders *docs, source* and *web*. The *docs* folder will contain content materials, including the sitemap and text files. The *source* folder will contain files used in the design of the Web site, such as PhotoShop, Illustrator and non-optimized image files.

All HTML pages and files that will be uploaded to the Web should be in the *web* folder. This folder serves as your development space before uploading files to the Web. Within the *web* folder, create a new HTML page and name it *index.html*. This is the standard default page on most Web servers and will serve as your home page. Create an *images* folder inside your *web* folder for all the optimized images on your site, as well as folders for your main content areas.

HTML is a set of tags that are inserted around the content in your files to tell the browser how to display your files. HTML stands for "hypertext markup language." Writing HTML does not require any special software; all you need is a text-editing program such as BBEdit or SimpleText that types plain text with no formatting. HTML tags tell the browser to make text big or small, to use a particular font, to get a picture, to build a table, and to create links to other files in your site or out somewhere in the World Wide Web.

HTML EDITORS are programs that allow you to create Web pages and manage Web sites without a strong knowledge of HTML. Two popular HTML editors are Macromedia Dreamweaver and Adobe GoLive. These programs provide a visual system to develop a Web page, import images, create links, add color, and set type. You can toggle back and forth between the visual design and the HTML code. We highly recommend working with an HTML editor, which can be easily learned through workshops and tutorials.

TABLES Many HTML pages use tables to create a structure and hierarchy within the code. Tables contain rows and columns. Each component in the table is called a cell. Inserting tables within cells is called nesting tables. Web designers manipulate tables to create orderly and interesting pages.

ACCESSIBILITY Visually impaired users employ automated screen readers that "linearize" Web pages into a continuous text that can be read aloud by a machine. Techniques for achieving accessibility include the captioning of all layout tables, the consistent use of "alt tags" (which identify image files), and the placement of page anchors in front of repeated navigation elements that enable users to go directly to the main content. Various software programs allow designers to test the linearization of their pages.

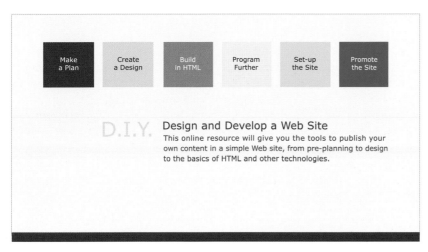

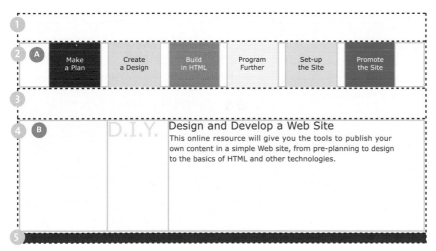

The master table has one column and five rows (numbered 1–5).

Tables A and B are nested inside master rows 2 and 4.

PLAIN VANILLA

This simple design was created in an HTML editor. Without adding any images, you can create interest with layout, shape, and color.

The first table we created has one column and five rows. Within rows 2 and 4, we nested tables A and B, holding cells for navigation and content. In order to control the height or width of a cell, insert a single-pixel transparent GIF and specify its size. This will prevent the cell from collapsing.

Verdana, a font designed by Matthew Carter for use on the Web, is used throughout the page. The header, navigation, body content, and contact information use different font sizes, creating a hierarchy of information.

The text in each navigation square links to interior pages within the site. These are called *relative links*. If a link points to a URL outside the local site, it is called an *absolute link*, and its link tag needs the full URL (http://...).

Design: Katherine Cornelius

The Maryland Institute College of Art Web site employs a variety of media, including Flash, Cold Fusion, JavaScript, and CSS. The navigation (created in Flash), the news items (created in Cold Fusion), and the photographic background image are all dynamically driven by a database. HTML is a container for the various elements.
Design: Carton Donofrio Interactive and Fast Spot

Beyond HTML

In many Web projects, HMTL is not enough. If you want to add a form, produce a blog, or even create a rollover image, you will need to employ additional Web technologies and scripting languages. Listed here are a few possible directions to pursue in creating interactive Web sites.

CSS (Cascading Style Sheet) is used to specify fonts, colors, headers, and positioning of text. Linked to your HMTL page in the <head> tag or embedded in the document, style sheets provide control and consistency throughout your site, especially with type. You can define styles for each font used on your site, and if you need to make changes to the size or color in the future, you only need to adjust the style sheet, not each individual page. HMTL editors, like Dreamweaver, make it easy to create and use style sheets.

JAVASCRIPT is a scripting language used to enhance Web pages, often executed by mouse functions, buttons, or other actions from the user. A simple navigation rollover is an example of JavaScript. You can use an HMTL editor to automatically generate JavaScript behaviors, or you can copy and paste desired code from existing Web sites.

MACROMEDIA FLASH is used for making animations, games, interactive menus, and other elements. You don't need this program to build an informational Web site, but it is fun to add motion to your pages. Flash is extremely powerful and complex, but creating simple animations is easy.

DYNAMIC WEB SITES use databases to supply content. A programming language such as ASP, ColdFusion, PHP, Perl or JSP is used to communicate with the database. As the user interacts with the site, dynamic Web pages are built on the fly.

This is also called a Content Management System. A CMS enables users to modify content through an administrative Web site, eliminating the need for content producers to have intimate knowledge of HTML.

OPEN SOURCE describes computer programs, scripting languages, and operating systems that use publicly available source code. In true D.I.Y. spirit, the open source philosophy encourages social interactivity. Programmers modify and improve the source code and then enter it back into the public domain. PHP is a popular open source scripting language that can be embedded into html.

XML (Extensible markup language) was created to solve the processing, presentation, and scalability issues associated with HTML. Using descriptive markup tags, such as <name>Katherine</name>, XML provides meaningful data that can be stored in a database. However, most browsers do not recognize XML. The Web standards commission, World Wide Web Consortium (W3C), developed XHTML to solve this problem.

XHTML (Extensible Hypertext Markup Language) is a combination of XML and HTML. Whereas HTML code can be written loosely, XHTML code follows strict guidelines. A true implementation across the Web will produce faster processing of Web pages and consistency of design across browsers.

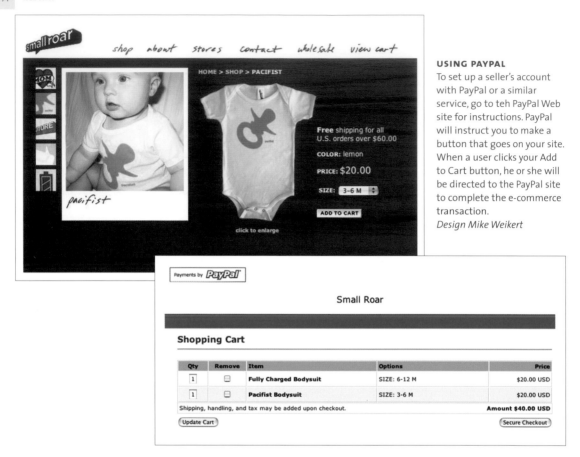

USING PAYPAL
To set up a seller's account with PayPal or a similar service, go to teh PayPal Web site for instructions. PayPal will instruct you to make a button that goes on your site. When a user clicks your Add to Cart button, he or she will be directed to the PayPal site to complete the e-commerce transaction.
Design Mike Weikert

Launching Your Site

DOMAIN NAME A domain name is a unique name that identifies a Web site, such as micadesign. org. When typed into a browser or sent as an e-mail address, the Domain Name System (DNS) translates micadesign.org into Internet Protocol (IP) numbers, such as 216.168.224.70. These numbers are used by the Internet to connect you to micadesign.org.

Domain name extensions include *.com, .net,* and *.org.* Many extensions are country-specific; for example the United Kingdom uses *.co.uk* and *.org. uk.*

REGISTERING A DOMAIN NAME When you choose a name for your Web site, check the *Whois* database located on a domain registry Web site to find out if the domain name is available. You can usually register the domain name at the same place where you purchase Web server space.

PURCHASE WEB SERVER SPACE To make your site public, you need a server, a dedicated computer that holds your Web site files and is available to users 24/7. You can rent space on a server for a relatively low cost per month. If your Web site uses programming other than HTML, the cost per month may be higher.

FTP File Transfer Protocol allows the transfer of files over the Internet or from one computer to another. When you buy Web server space, the hosting company will provide you an FTP address or another method of transferring your files to the Web.

E-COMMERCE If you intend to sell items on your Web site, you will need a merchant account and shopping cart capability. You can build your own shopping cart with a programming language, or you can rent space from a network-based e-commerce service. One popular method for transactions is PayPal. Remember that once an item sells, you will have to produce the item and plan a method for shipping.

SEARCH ENGINE OPTIMIZATION There are several ways that you can optimize your Web site in order to boost its ranking in search engines. Of course, nothing guarantees that you will be listed at the top, but it's a good start.

There are numerous companies that will submit your Web site to search engines for a fee. Since this is a time-consuming process, purchasing this service may be a helpful option. Type in "Search Engine Optimization" on a search page to find providers. Otherwise, go to the major search engines and learn how you can submit your site.

Several search engines, such as Google, rank Web pages by the number of links pointing to the site. The Web crawlers also look at the text around the links and the link popularity of the referral Web site. Find Web sites that have similar content and ask them to list your Web site. Often times you can list their Web site in return.

MARKETING Look at the list of audiences that you created at the beginning of the Web development process. How can you best reach these audiences? What sites do they visit on the Web? What keywords will they type into a search engine?

You can use this information to create targeted advertisements on search engines. If you have a list of email subscribers, you may also want to research email blasts.

OPTIZMIZE YOUR WEB SITE

• Create unique, descriptive titles for every page on your site, such as "DIY Shirt Designs." Since Web crawlers only search the first 50-80 characters, be short and concise. Do not use punctuation or special characters in the title. Make sure the content of the page is relevant to the title.

• Include meta tags (key words that describe a page's content) in your HTML document. Although this is not as important as it used to be, having descriptive keywords is still beneficial. You want to be sure that the keywords are relevant to your content.

• Fix broken links. Web crawlers will not index your whole site if there are broken links.

• If you want your images to be read by search engines, add alt tags, which are text descriptions of the images in your site, including images that serve as navigation.

Zines

Allen Harrison

Zines cover a spectrum of topics, from fanzines about the latest Buffy episode, to instructional zines about stealing copies from Kinkos, to personal zines about the adventures of substitute teaching. This eclectic discourse nourishes the creation of subcultures. With an estimated 25,000 titles in existence, zines have become a socially significant force. Few zine publishers make monetary profit from their work, yet they invest considerable amounts of money and time publishing their projects. Zines sustain a spirit of independence and an often confrontational relationship with mainstream media.

WHY PUBLISH? Publishing is fun: it involves collaboration, writing, creativity, artwork, and getting surprise packages in the mail. Zines help zine makers connect with interesting people sharing a common interest. Zinesters use the conferences and the Internet to form and coordinate underground networks that link zine makers around the world. The zine community is rooted in the concept of trade. Many zine makers trade their zines for other zines, using their publications as a form of currency and a tool for networking.

FRICTION MAGAZINE
Design: Allen Harrison
Cover photography:
Melissa Hostetler
Still life photograph:
Nancy Froehlich

PLANNING YOUR ZINE

- *What type of zine will you create (personal, political, artist-made)?*

- *Will there be a theme? Planning an overall topic and attitude for your writings will help create a cohesive zine.*

- *What is your budget?*

- *Who is your audience?*

- *Who will contribute content?*

- *How many copies will you make?*

- *What is your schedule for writing, editing, designing, printing, and distributing your zine?*

- *What are your output options (home printer, copy center, fax machine, e-mail)?*

PROMOTING YOUR ZINE

- *Create a web site that promotes and sells your zine. Use Paypal or CCnow to handle credit card and processing if you don't have a merchant account.*

- *Collect e-mail addresses and create an e-newsletter promoting your project.*

- *Attend zine events and lecture at workshops.*

- *Create stickers, buttons, patches, flyers, and postcards.*

- *Work with other zines; trade ads, reviews, etc.*

- *Have a release party.*

- *Create a free content sampler.*

- *Contact local and national press related to zines.*

- *Create cool giveaways (stickers, pencils, coasters).*

SHORT-RUN PUBLICATION

up to 1000 copies

LAYOUT Do you have access to a computer? Many zinesters still use a traditional cut-and paste method for producing layouts.

PAGE STRUCTURE Consider using a basic grid to bring order to your pages. (See our NEWSLETTER chapter for more information about grids.)

TYPOGRAPHY Less is often more when working with type faces. Choose a type family with varying weights to create heirarchy and contrast for your page. Devise a system of headers, decks, body copy, and footers to achieve a consistent look thoughout your zine.

IMAGES Choose imagery that helps tell the story. Avoid violating copyright laws by using your own art or work by people you know.

TRIM SIZE The format of a short-run zine is usually derived from a standard letter- or legal-sized page. For example, a quarter-sheet zine (4 1/4 x 5 1/2 inches) is based on 8 1/2-x-11-inch stock.

BINDING Many short-run zines are stapled through the inside seam (saddle-wired). This can be done by a copy center or commercial printer, or you can do it yourself with a long-necked stapler available from an office supplier. (See our BOOK chapters for more binding ideas.)

COVER STOCK You can choose cover stock from your local copy center, but you will be able to find more interesting (and economical) materials by searching on-line for overstocked paper. A local printer may have leftover paper you can use.

PRINT PRODUCTION Laser printing is the highest-quality reproduction method for short-run printing. Photocopying works well from cut-and-paste layouts. Put your spreads together so that they will come out in the right order when they are printed back to back and stapled together. (See our NEWSLETTER chapter for more information on printer's spreads). When you have all your copies made, have a pizza party and get your friends to help assemble your zine.

THIS IS THE ZINE: *Rutger Wolfson*
ON THE VERGE OF SUMMER: *Rachel Hartman*
PRAXIS: *Jason Kucsma*
PENSACOLA: *Candy*
CREMEFILLED: *Jessica*

7 THINGS TO CONSIDER

WHAT IS THE FOCUS?

Why do you WANT TO MAKE A ZINE?

how will you distribute your zine?

WOULD YOU CONTINUE TO DO IT IF NOBODY bought it?

Will you TAKE WRITING AND ART CONTRIBUTIONS?

how will you produce the zine?

Is IT WORTH YOUR TIME AND MONEY?

MEDIUM-RUN PUBLICATION

1,000 to 5,000 copies

Like many zines, *Friction* magazine started as a side project during college. After creating three print issues ranging from 250 to 1,000 copies, the editors decided to take our publication to the Web in 2001. Publishing on the Web, *Friction* accumulated close to 400 articles, a great core of talent, and a steady audience within two years. The Web site was used to conduct a survey with readers and contributors to see if there would be interest in a print version of the magazine. The response was positive, so *Friction* created a print version that featured the best work of its most promising and consistent contributors.

PUBLISHING A MEDIUM-RUN ZINE

• Work with your illustrators and photographers to develop an overall look and feel for the magazine that will compliment the artwork. Their input will help build a sense of community around the project.

• Find a printing company with previous D.I.Y. zine experience. Using word-of-mouth recommendations, contact several printers and look at samples of their work.

• Get bids (printing estimates) from a few different printers. Printers can advise you on the paper stock for content pages and for the cover. The price of printing your zine will be affected by your choice of paper and use of color.

• If you want your zine to be distributed to bookstores, you will need a UPC barcode or an ISBN number. Do a search on the Internet for Web sites that provide instant barcodes or ISBN numbers in EPS format for download.

• Advertising can be a crucial source of revenue. Make a list of potential advertisers (record labels, distributors, Web sites, bands) that have ties to your audience.

• Design postcards with ad rates, sizes, and deadlines, and send them to potential advertisers. A sales representative can work on commission and help you create extra materials such as one-sheets and giveaways.

• Assemble a list of independent bookstores and zine distributors to whom you can send promotional copies with a terms document. Some stores will buy copies from you outright; others will sell them on consignment.

FRICTION MAGAZINE
Design: Allen Harrison
Cover illustration:
Rama Hughes
Still life photograph:
Dan Meyers

Interviews

Leia Bell

Nicholas Blechman

Matthew Peterson

Christopher Sleboda

Todd St. John

Nolen Strals and Bruce Willen

Speak Up

Interviewed by Josh Malinow

Built to Spill & DRAW
May 14th
at Bricks*
doors 7:30
* a private club for members
Tickets 12$.

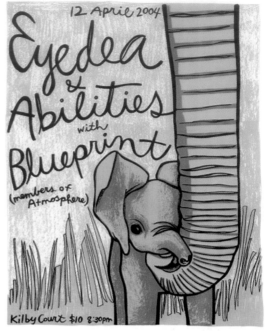

12 Aprile 2004
Eyedea & Abilities
with
Blueprint
(members of Atmosphere)
Kilby Court $10 8:30pm

Kilby Court's 5th Anniversary
featuring:
Guitorchestra
Tolchock Trio
In Camera
Take the Fall
& Hudson River School
July 23, 2004
7:30 $6

The Jealous Sound
Armor for Sleep &
a Barbeque hosted by the Rock Salt
29 August 2003
at Kilby Court

Kilby Court presents
The Decemberists & the Long Winters
May 31, 2004
at Lo-fi Café in SLC
$10 8 o'clock

Leia Bell

Leia Bell is a poster designer and printer in Utah.
www.leiabell.com

How did you get involved with design and printing?

My high school art teacher ran his own printing business before switching to public schools, so he set up his old screen printing equipment in the classroom. I was hooked by the time I was about fifteen. I started printing t-shirts for friends' bands, covering my parents' driveway with drying shirts. I would also make Xerox flyers for punk shows in my home town. It was all cut-and-paste style—I didn't have a computer. I moved to Utah in 1997 and enrolled in the University of Utah. I wanted to study graphic design, but my portfolio was rejected, so I opted for printmaking.

How did you get involved with concert posters?

After graduating, I assumed that I would never use my printing degree. I was working a minimum-wage job when I became friends with Phil, the owner of an all-ages venue here in Salt Lake City that I frequented called Kilby Court. I offered to make flyers for him, starting out with black-and-white Xerox handbills. When Phil discovered that I knew how to screen print, he suggested that I make limited-edition posters for all of the shows. He built me a little printing studio next to the venue and I got started. I had a recognizable style, so the small, colorful posters became a sort of trademark for the venue. People could look at the posters and instantly know they were for a Kilby Court show.

What do you find appealing about designing, lettering, and screen printing your posters by hand?

I enjoy the physicality. I love to get my hands dirty and hold up a poster and know that I was a part of the process from start to finish. I am a printing junkie. I want to hurry and get drawings done so I can get to the printing. Once I lay down the first color on a poster, I can't wait to see what the next one will look like. I've never been big on computers. I mainly just use mine to check e-mail and scan my finished posters so I can post them on my Web site.

You project a distinctly human quality in your work. Where do you find your inspiration?

Most of my images are based on photographs taken of people I know, kids hanging out at parties or the Kilby Court shows. I am fairly shy, so when I am in a public place I bring my camera with me, to hide behind. I am a people-watcher, and I like to study mannerisms and facial expressions. When I get my photos back home, I draw them, editing out the unnecessary bits of information and simplifying the scene to something universal that anyone can relate to. I have often heard that my images of people remind the viewer of someone they know.

How can someone get started designing and screen printing posters?

When I started screen printing the Kilby Court flyers, I was pretty much penniless. I saved up to get just the basics. I found some discarded screens and restretched them myself, got scraps of paper from a friend who worked at a large printing warehouse, got trashed squeegees from the university and had them sanded down, and printed with mistint latex paints instead of inks. The most pricey thing I bought was a power washer to clean out the screens. The other expensive thing was a paper cutter. My very first set up was around $200. The best advice I think I can give is to apprentice with someone first, especially if you haven't done printing in school. Don't spend a lot of money and then discover you hate the process of printing—it's not for everyone.

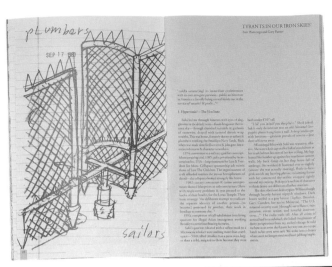

Nicholas Blechman

Nicholas Blechman is a graphic designer, illustrator and art director. He is the founder and editor of *Nozone*, an independent magazine of politics and culture.
www.knickerbockerdesign.com

How did you get involved with design, illustration and publishing?

Pretty much through *Nozone*. Publishing my own magazine was my school, and it was a trial-by-error experiece. I made lots of mistakes along the way, but that was part of the process of learning design. I also got my education by looking at other magazines and zines. A lot of Xeroxed magazines were being sent through the mail during the late 1980s and early 1990s. There was never a real sense of, "I have to know graphic design in order to do this," or "I have to go to school in order to do this." It was all just, "This is how I feel, this is what I want to say, and let's do it."

My father was a cartoonist [R. O. Blechman], and he always loved graphic design, so that was my education, too. I was brought up in an environment where I was surrounded by illustration and graphic design. I was always aware of it.

I was also influenced by posters and fliers for punk bands, like the Dead Kennedys. The people who were making those posters were not commercial artists. And it all looked cool. In a weird way, the worse it looked, the cooler it was. Any polish or any kind of formal design aesthetic was almost viewed as a hinderance.

You work as an illustrator, designer, art director, and an editor. Do you consider yourself more of one than the others, or are they all interrelated?

They're really all interrelated. One of the elements of doing-it-yourself is that work isn't broken down into different professional categories. You'll end up doing a lot of different jobs to make a project happen.

What moved you to create and publish *Nozone*?

At the time, I was feeling politically desperate. I was motivated by a genuine concern with the state of the planet, and I wanted to find a graphic outlet for my anxieties and frustrations. Doing my own magazine was my rallying cry. It was a way to express my opinions and to involve others.

Given the power of the Internet, why does *Nozone* continue to exist in print?

I'm sure I could reach a larger number of people on the Internet, but I feel that if I devote so much work to the project, I want it to result in a book that I can hold and carry around. There is something important about the weight of a book, the texture, and how it feels. Would the *Communist Manifesto* have had the same impact if it had been published on the Web? Because it's a book, because you can hit somebody over the head with it, it has physical presence. The Web has a temporary, transient quality, whereas books are permanent. Books stay on your bookshelf and they stay with you.

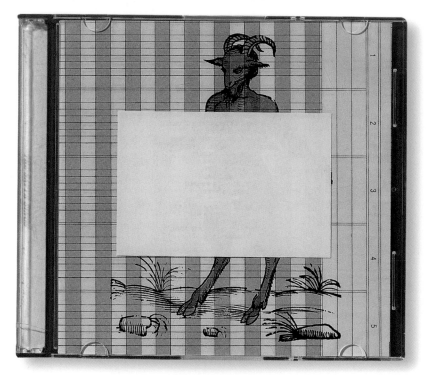

Matthew Peterson

Matthew Peterson is a graphic desinger in Chicago. In his
spare time, he makes mix CDs for friends and family.

What do you find compelling about graphic design?

I don't see any inherent promise in graphic design
itself. It's just a description of certain tools and
characteristics. But we designers do succeed
at times in making beautiful, resonant things
that compel thought. We succeed in spite of the
limitations of our trade, not because of its inherent
potential. An acute idea, alone and unmade, is
where we find our promise.

Aside from your professional practice, you also design graphics and packaging for mix CDs that you make for friends and family. What inspires you to take the time and effort to do this?

I can't stand a plain CD. I need some sort of entry
into the music, and the package serves as that.
We want to improve our abilities. We want our
lives to get better. We hope we're taking steps that
will translate into greater happiness. So, when the
first mix tapes I made were just Maxell sleeves
marked with a Sharpie, I wanted the handwriting
to get more refined. When the handwriting wasn't
improving fast enough, I started printing the text
and cutting up magazines. And so on.

What are the differences in designing graphics for a professional album and for a personal mix?

One comes from the outside. It's a considered
reaction, and it arrives through a repeatable process.
The other comes from the gut. It's like a twitch.
It's been enabled by the design process developed
for professional work, but only in the sense that
past experience has built a better intuition, a more
accomplished gut.

Commercially recorded music seems poised to shed its physical casing in exchange for a completely digital existence. What are your thoughts about the future of music packaging?

We are largely visual beasts. Packaging has an
impact on our assessment of individual albums.
If you remove that physical component, the music
is left alone, naked and sweaty, and it has to speak
for itself. Design might, in a way, do a disservice to
music by affecting our idea of it from the outside.
Personally, I'm inclined to think: design it. Of course,
I have a vested interest.

What advice would you share with someone who is interested in designing packaging for mix CDs?

I've never felt worthy of advising. But let's try, and
say that just like love and your forty-hour work
week: Be careful who you give it to.

Christopher Sleboda

Christopher Sleboda is a graphic designer
and illustrator in Connecticut.
www.gluekit.com

How did you get involved with design and illustration?

When I was in high school, I discovered hand-made
hardcore and punk rock fanzines. I loved their
rawness and immediacy, and I also liked how the
design of a zine reflected the author's personality.
Anything could be said, and anything could be done.
It's a great form of expression. I started to make
my own zines and loved the craft—using Xerox
machines, typewriter text, collaged photos.

When I began studying design in college, I
also started designing and selling t-shirts. I made
shirts that I wanted to wear and that no one else
was making. Then I made catalogs, mailed them
out, and orders came pouring in. At the same time
I also began designing record and CD covers. I
would design something for a friend's band, and
then another band would see it and want me to
do something for them. Since college, I continued
doing freelance work, taught design, and recently
finished my MFA in Graphic Design at Yale.

What do you find compelling about graphic design as a way to express yourself?

Graphic design is like throwing a brick—the impact
is immediate. I find it amazing that something can
be communicated in a matter of seconds, and it can
have so many levels of meaning. And I'm constantly
drawn to images and graphics of all kinds. There is
just something so powerful about them that I have
to be involved in their creation.

Much of your work achieves a handmade aesthetic. How do you use the computer as a tool, but still maintain a "lo-tech" look?

It relates back to making fanzines and the craft of
making something with your hands. Revealing the

hand and leaving evidence of the process within the
image is a big part of my work. I also enjoy finding
interesting imperfections that reveal themselves
in the process and seeing these imperfections as
beautiful mistakes. I like to think of Gluekit (my
Web site and design practice) as a collision of
fragments or an accident on purpose.

Besides working for clients, you also design products, like t-shirts and tote bags, that feature your graphics. What inspired you to design your own products?

The satisfaction of bringing a product to life and
making it real. If there is something I want that
doesn't exist, it's the perfect opportunity to make
it. Creating something allows you to contribute to
culture and to have a conversation with the world
around you.

What advice would you give someone who wants to use graphic design as a tool for sharing ideas?

Go for it. Start with something small and then stick
with it. And take risks. Don't play it too safe.

Todd St. John

Todd St. John is a graphic designer living in New York. He directs music videos and designs original products through his companies Green Lady (founded with Gary Bezel) and HunterGatherer. www.huntergatherer.net

How did you get involved with design and illustration?

I thought about going to film school, or art school, or studying music. Graphic design wasn't necessarily the perfect fit, but it brought together a lot of things I was interested in. You can call yourself a graphic designer and work with musicians, work with animation, work with video, work with print. It's wide open.

Graphic design is also a democratic medium. It's public and accessible. Some of the things that affected me as a teenager and a young person came through mass media. The idea that something can make an impact and speak to a large number of people is rewarding.

Graphic design is a shared language, and since you're speaking in a shared language, you can play with that language. You can play against certain assumptions that are built in to it, and you can play against symbols.

You've referred to graphic design as "the language of legitimacy." What do you mean?

Design lets people know that whatever it is you are talking about has been considered and planned out. It looks right and it looks like people have put thought into it. When you make something concrete, like making a flier for a show that your band is playing, it can make the event seem more real, more concrete, and more relevant. Graphic design comes in many forms. Whether you're making an annual report, or a logo, or a t-shirt, design imbues a kind of legitimacy to its subject.

What are the different challenges involved in working on your own products as compared to working on projects for clients?

With a client, an automatic expectation is built into the process. The parameters have largely been defined before you get the project. With my own work, the hardest thing is setting those parameters for myself. A lot of times, I'll deliberately try to set some of those parameters. I like the collaborative client process, so I try to reconstruct that.

What advice would you share with people who want to use graphic design as a tool for creating their own products?

Graphic design is about the overall impression. When you're creating a product, think about it in terms of creating a brand. Think about the entire experience—not just the product, but also everything that goes with it and how it's presented. Extend beyond the product and reinforce it.

Nolen Strals and Bruce Willen

Nolen Strals and Bruce Willen have day jobs in Baltimore as well as their independent design outfit, Post Typography. They are members of Double Dagger, one of the world's only "designcore" punk rock bands. www.posttypography.com, www.doubledagger.com

When did you start working together?

NS: We were both students at MICA. I was working in the mailroom, and Bruce came in one day and said, "Do you want to start a metal band?" And I thought that would be cool, so we tried to start a metal band, but we didn't really know how to play metal, so it ended up being this crazy hardcore band called League of Death. We practiced for a couple of months, and we thought it would be cool to make a poster for our first show, so we snuck into the mailroom one night and cut pictures out of an old book and magazine, and drew some lettering, and stayed up all night printing.

And you still play in a band together.

NS: After League of Death broke up, I was in the mailroom again and Bruce came in and said, "Do you want to start a band that writes songs about graphic design?" And I thought that sounded cool. That's how Double Dagger started.

BW: We started getting asked to do work for people who had seen posters we made for our shows.

You screen print posters yourselves. Is it gratifying to work with your hands?

NS: After sitting all day in a cubicle, there's a satisfaction that comes from working at three in the morning, when my back is sore from pulling prints.

What do you find compelling about graphic design?

NS: Design gets out to the public. In school, my fine art work was only seen by my teachers and classmates, and then it was kind of *dead*. But if you design something, like a t-shirt or poster, it goes out into society and has this life outside of you.

What advice do you have for people who want to use graphic design to promote their band or music?

BW: Think about what distinguishes your music and how you can translate your musical concepts into visuals. Don't get caught up in the technology. Focus on the idea.

Speak Up

Armin Vit and Byrony Gomez-Palacio are the editors and producers of Speak Up, one of the first and most influential design blogs. www.underconsideration.com/speakup

How did you get involved with design?

AV: One day my dad—a mathematician by education and a businessman by day—brought home one of the very first Macintosh computers and Illustrator 1.0. He loved the fact that he could "do" things, so he re-enrolled in college at the age of 50 to study graphic design part-time. He bought books and subscribed to magazines and by the time I started college, I already had an amazing library at home. And a Mac.

My formal education, from a nice university in Mexico, is in traditional print and identity design. I was the last generation to be taught how to do mechanicals, and not a day passed that I was not forced to use French curves, rapidographs, and even gouache.

BGP: One of my teachers in high school decided to teach us about graphic design instead of the traditional art course. She introduced me to rapidographs and vellum, gouche and illustration board. It was through her that my interest grew to the point of enrolling at the Universidad Iberoamericana a couple years later.

What do you find compelling about graphic design as a way to express yourself?

AV: I still have trouble thinking of graphic design as a mode of self-expression. Self-initiated projects can have that potential, but graphic design as a service to a client is different. Sure, we instill design with our own visual sensibilities, imagination, and experiences, but the goal is to express somebody else's product or service.

What inspired you to create Speak Up?

AV: Now I look back and laugh, but Speak Up was inspired by me being pissed off. When I got out of college, I stepped right into the dot-com boom and saw hundreds of people starting to call themselves designers just because they knew how to write HTML and animate in Flash. With the Web came a new generation of designers more interested in snazzy form than anything else, and it came with Web sites to support it. Self-ascribed "design portals" were popping up, and it was a visual link-fest, which is all well and good, but I found the "design" attribution to be disturbing.

Initially, Speak Up was a reaction to that. It was to be a Web site for traditional designers, where, in my own silly words, we could talk about "real" design. The first version of Speak Up didn't get much attention, but it served as a foundation for what I wanted to create: a medium to talk freely, passionately, and honestly about graphic design.

BGP: Although I was part of it from the beginning, it wasn't until I realized just how much Speak Up was to become part of our daily lives that I decided to become more active. I left my back-stage status, and joined the forces on the front line.

How did being a graphic designer affect the way you approached creating Speak Up?

AV: I wanted it to look good. When I first transformed Speak Up to blog format, a lot of people said that it was "print-like," and that was one of my goals. I was trained as a print designer, but the first two years of my career were an on-the-job education in Web design and programming, so I was able to put together both for SpeakUp.

What work is involved with running Speak Up?

AV: Speak Up is really a 24-hour a day job. It is on my mind all day, every day. I devote a good three to five hours a day during the work week. This means late nights, early mornings, and short lunches so that I can also manage to get some other work done. Chores include answering e-mails, fixing people's comments, uploading news and events, and fielding suggestions for discussions. When we are selling something, there is a lot of customer-service. On the weekends, I write posts or make improvements to the site or work on spin off projects. Weekends are also when Byrony and I sit down for a few hours and discuss Speak Up. We talk about what we want to do, what are we doing okay, and what are we screwing up. Then we discuss what to make for dinner. In essence, it becomes a juggling act between real-life and blog-life. Luckily, I think, both are merging into a well-functioning-life.

BGP: My main focus is Word It, the visual blogging section of Speak Up. I can't participate during the working hours of the day, which gears my involvement to management and administrative issues. I am the bad cop in this partnership, the one with deadlines, reality checks, bank statements, and logistics in her bag.

What advice would you share with someone who wants to create a blog?

AV: Stand for something and be passionate about it. Don't try to be all things to all people because you can't. Have patience and perseverance. Find an angle that no one else has. And most of all, believe in it. If you don't, no one will.

**GRAPHIC DESIGN
MFA PROGRAM
MARYLAND INSTITUTE
COLLEGE OF ART
2005/2006**

Kimberly Bost

Michelle Brooks

Katherine Cornelius

Alissa Faden

Nancy Froehlich

Allen Harrison

J. Spence Holman

Christoper Jackson

Ellen Lupton

Josh Malinow

George Moore

Adam Palmer

Jennifer Cole Phillips

Jessica Pilar Rodríguez

Zvezdana Rogic

Veronica Semeco Rojas

Kristen Spilman

Mike Weikert

Ida Woldemichael

KIMBERLY BOST has been an artist since conception. She received her BFA from the University of North Carolina at Greensboro.

MICHELLE BROOKS studied photography and installation arts at Bard College before studying design at MICA. When not plugged into a computer, she likes to knit, read books about dragons, and dig around in the garden.

KATHERINE CORNELIUS works her muscles by running marathons, playing soccer, and hiking, and her mind by doing graphic design. She was a senior Web designer in Washington, DC, before coming to MICA.

ALISSA FADEN is a designer, art historian, trendspotter, and writer in one creatively-wrapped package. Her goal is to earn her fifteen minutes by coming up with the next big thing.

NANCY FROEHLICH studied history and photography at University of Washington in Seattle. By day she can be found behind a camera lens, in front of a computer, or teaching design. By night she lets loose on the dance floor.

DAVINA GRUNSTEIN received her BA from UCLA in English Literature and her MFA from UC Davis in Fine Art. She is interested in the overlap between art and design—graphic, environmental, product, and fashion.

ALLEN HARRISON is creative director of Static Spark Interactive and art director of *Friction* Magazine, an online/print publication started in 2001. *Friction* has been recognized by *Print*, The Addy Awards, Mother Jones, Yahoo, and *The Nation*. He teaches design courses at MICA.

J. SPENCE HOLMAN is from Baltimore and likes to make stuff. He graduated from Vassar College, where he made different stuff.

CHRISTOPHER JACKSON was born in Dalton, GA, the carpet capital of the world, and earned a BFA in Painting and Drawing from The University of Tennessee at Chattanooga. He was recently appointed to the design faculty at Emmanuel College in Boston.

ELLEN LUPTON has written numerous books on design. She has taught at MICA since 1997, where she is the founding director of the graphic design MFA program. She also serves as curator of contemporary design at Cooper-Hewitt, National Design Museum.

JOSH MALINOW has a background in fiction and nonfiction writing. His written work has appeared in various publications, including MAD Magazine. He holds a BA in journalism from the University of Maryland-College Park.

GEORGE MOORE is a roaming buffalo, going wherever motion graphics will take him. He is currently teaching motion graphics and interactive design at St. Mary's College in southern Maryland.

ADAM PALMER grew up in Seaford, Delaware and studied graphic design at Salisbury University in Maryland. Since arriving at MICA, Adam has had numerous illustrations featured in the *New York Times* "Week in Review." Music consumes the rest of his life.

JENNIFER COLE PHILLIPS has an MFA from Rhode Island School of Design and has taught at MICA and the University of Baltimore. Her work has been included in the annuals of *Graphis Design*, *Graphis Poster*, *Print*, the Art Director's Clubs of Metropolitan Washington and New York, AIGA 50, and the ACD 100 Show, among others.

JESSICA P. RODRÍGUEZ was born and raised in San Juan, Puerto Rico. She worked as a senior designer at a Washington, D.C. studio for five years and is currently developing a line of original pattern designs, intended for use by fabric or paper product companies.

ZVEZDANA ROGIC runs her own fashion label, Zvezdana, and teaches graphic design at MICA. She loves to collaborate, write fiction, and work out. Hailing from Serbia, she speaks with a deep Mittel-European accent.

VERONICA SEMECO was born and raised in Valencia, Venezuela. She interned at the National Museum of Natural History, Smithsonian Institution. She is currently initiating a business designing and importing Venezuelan handcrafts.

KRISTEN SPILMAN studied graphic design at Boston University and worked professionally in the D.C. area before attending MICA. Her work is inspired by architecture, fashion, and typography. She recently joined the staff at Pentagram Design.

MIKE WEIKERT earned his BFA in graphic design from Miami University. He was creative director at Atlanta-based Iconologic and served as a design consultant to the International Olympic Committee. He is currently co-chair of the graphic design department at MICA and runs Small Roar, a baby clothing line, with his wife Stephannie.

IDA WOLDEMICHAEL grew up in Arlington, Virginia, but stays close to her native Eritrean culture. She has interned at Wolf Trap, The Corcoran Gallery of Art, and Visual Design Studio 4, and she has worked as a designer for *Urbanite* magazine in Baltimore.

RESOURCES

WWW.PAPER-SOURCE.COM This is an excellent resource for paper and book binding materials. They also have great ideas for invitation designs and supply a great variety of colored envelopes with matching papers.

PRINT GOCCO This low-cost, low-mess, low-tech silkscreen system is ideally suited to short-run printing on paper or cardboard. You can also print on fabric with Print Gocco, but expect an irregular result with a handmade feel. Print area is small (approximately 4 x 6 inches). Available from www. welshproducts.com.

GBC PROCLICK BINDING SYSTEM No bigger than a three-hole punch, the ProClick binder punches a row of tiny holes along the edge of a stack of paper; finish the job with a click-on black plastic spine. Unlike ugly binding "combs," ProClick spines are reasonably sleek, and the resulting booklet lies flat. Available on-line from office discounters.

WWW.SEVENGYPSIES.COM This company specializes in interesting hardware for paper crafts. Check out the beautiful metal index tabs, card holders, brass tags, and binding rings.

WWW.GIFTBOWTIQUE.COM If you are interested in mail-order machine embroidery, this company provides an amazing range of monogram styles and thread colors.

WWW.PHILOBIBLON.COM ("The Book Arts Web") This is a good source of information about bookbinding trends, techniques, and events; numerous links to useful tutorials.

WWW.SUBLIMESTITCHING.COM Published by needlework designer Jenny Hart, this Web site promotes Hart's surprising embroidery patterns (from "Monkey Love" to a skull and crossbones). The site provides general how-to information as well as access to Hart's own kits, patterns, and supplies.

WWW.DIYNET.COM The DIY Network provides infor–mation on a variety of projects, ranging from moving tips to restoring an old Harley. The Tutorial section is very thorough and helpful, although you do have to sit through an occasional ad from their sponsors.

WWW.WEBMONKEY.COM This Web site is a great tool for Web developers of all levels, supplying easy-to-follow tutorials in design, multimedia, e-commerce, and programming.

WEBMONKEY FOR KIDS http://webmonkey.wired.com/webmonkey/kids/index.html This is a useful how-to site aimed at kids and teachers.

WWW.LYNDA.COM Another useful site for Web tips and tutorials.

WWW.READYMADEMAG.COM *ReadyMade* is a bi-monthly print magazine for people who like to make stuff. Most featured projects focus on repurposing everyday objects. Check out the Forum section online for additional ideas.

WWW.FLICKR.COM A resource of amateur photography with free hi-res downloads. Don't be surprised if you stumble upon some pretty decent work.

WWW.COCKTAILDB.COM Drink-It-Yourself! A D.I.Y. guide to making cocktails.

ART SUPPLIES
www.dickblick.com
www.engineersupply.com
www.pearlpaint.com
www.charrette.com
www.flaxart.com

ARCHIVAL MATERIALS
www.archival.com
ww.exposuresonline.com
www.lightimpressionsdirect.com
www.metaledgeinc.com

BOXES, CARTONS, PLASTICS, PACKING SUPPLIES
www.papermart.com
www.uline.com
www.consolidatedplastics.com

COMMERCIAL PAPER RESOURCES
www.gilbertpaper.com
www.mrfrench.com
www.curiouscollection.com
www.crane.com
www.mohawkpaper.com
www.internationalpaper.com
www.gmund.com
www.finchpaper.com
www.wausaupapers.com
www.neenahpaper.com

CULTURE, TRENDS, MARKETPLACE
www.designboom.com
www.joshrubin.com
www.dailycandy.com
www.urbanfreeflow.com
www.trendwatching.com
www.fabric8.com